SAVING
Savvy

PRESENTS

SAVING
Savvy

Smart and easy ways to
CUT YOUR SPENDING IN HALF
and raise your standard of living . . . and giving!

Kelly Hancock

WORTHY
PUBLISHING

Published by Worthy Publishing, a division of Worthy Media, Inc., 134 Franklin Road, Suite 200, Brentwood, Tennessee 37027.

HELPING PEOPLE EXPERIENCE THE HEART OF GOD

eBook available at www.worthypublishing.com

Audio distributed through Oasis Audio; visit www.oasisaudio.com

Library of Congress Control Number: 2011931411

For foreign and subsidiary rights, contact Riggins International Rights Services, Inc.; www.rigginsrights.com

Published in association with the literary agency of Daniel Literary Group, LLC, Nashville, TN 37215.

ISBN: 978-1-936034-53-6 (trade paper)

Cover Design: Chris Tobias, www.tobiasdesign.com
Cover Background Pattern: © John Rawsterne/iStockphoto.com
Interior Design and Typesetting: Susan Browne Design

Printed in the United States of America

11 12 13 14 15 LBM 8 7 6 5 4 3 2 1

Contents

Acknowledgments

In sincere appreciation, I want to thank Byron Williamson and Rob Birkhead of Worthy Publishing for believing in me and *Saving Savvy*. Also, a special thanks to Kris Bearss and Jennifer Stair, for guiding me through the editing process with enthusiasm and grace, and to Greg Daniel, my literary agent.

This book would not have been possible had it not been for Rebekah Cook inviting me into her home to show me that this was possible—thank you. And Rebecca Ingram Powell, who flat-out told me I needed to write this book, and provided encouragement and counsel along the way. You, my dear friend, are so precious to me.

I am indebted to Greg Fritz, Jim Selby, Henry Williams, Derek Bell, Marty Reed, Kelly Sutton, Cheryl Fritz, Julie Gillies, Gretchen Vaught, Jennifer Briggs, Erin Chase, Chris Copley, Jeanne Bergstrom, Susie Hardin, Steve NeSmith, Chris Thomas, Jack Galloway, Neal Webb, Thom Chittom, Sherry Smothermon-Short, Josh and Bethany Newman of St8mnt, and Michael Clarke of Uncorrupted.net. All of you helped in ways you will never know. You are a blessing.

Thanks to my community group—Billy, Pennie, Ben, Rhondi, Jacqueline, Scott, Cari, Laura, Scott, and Melissa—for listening to my story and supporting me.

A special thank you to Ellen, Zach, Larry, and Rhonda for giving selflessly of your time to watch Ainsley and Garrett, so I could have time to write and edit this book. It was such a comfort to know my children were being so well taken care of by those who love them most.

To my precious children, Ainsley and Garrett, for being who God made you to be. You give me joy and encouragement every day.

And to my husband, Bradford, I give my most heartfelt thanks and deepest love. You have helped me in editing, juggling schedules, and you've supported me every step of the way. Even when I thought I couldn't do it, you always knew I could. You are the most selfless, supportive, and loving husband anyone could dream of. I love you dearly and feel honored to be able to walk this road with you.

Lastly, but most importantly, I want to thank my Lord and Savior, Jesus Christ. Daily You amaze me in Your ways: the way You create, orchestrate, and have Your hand on every single detail. This book is for You, Lord; thank You for giving me the opportunity to serve You.

Introduction

. . . .

MY STORY

A few years ago, my life was very different.

I was a top-performing sales rep for a Fortune 500 company. I loved my job and had plans for my career. Training? Marketing? Management? The options were endless. I knew if I worked hard, I would get results.

When I became pregnant with my first child, I had no intention of quitting work to stay at home. Why should I? The money was good, I was successful, and the work stimulated me. I felt that I would be giving up an important part of myself if I stayed home, and that wouldn't be good for me *or* my baby. Besides, my husband, Bradford, and I had purchased a home that required both our incomes to make our mortgage payment. So leaving my job was simply not an option.

After our daughter was born, I felt the Lord tugging at my heart to take a leap of faith and leave my high-paying job. This was no easy decision because I brought home half of our income. Would our family have enough money to live on without my income? Though I wanted to follow the Lord's leading for my family, I dreaded the financial impact on our lives. I knew that statistics show more than half of marriages end in divorce, with money problems playing a major role. Who needs that kind of financial pressure?

So I went back to work. Yet after two months back in the office, I just couldn't shake the tug in my heart that the Lord wanted me to be an at-home mom. My husband and I discussed it at length and decided I would give my two-week notice. Through that incredibly risky step, I began to see an opportunity for God to supernaturally meet our needs in practical, day-to-day ways.

When Bradford and I worked out our first one-income budget, we were stunned to discover how much money we were wasting each month on nonessentials! We thought we were good about not overspending, but we realized we could do a much better job. Not only were we paying full price for our groceries, cleaning supplies, and toiletries, but we were spending far too much on other things like dining out.

My husband's income was going to need to stretch further, and God provided a dear friend, Rebekah, to serve as my savings mentor. She introduced me to a new way of saving through shopping sales, stocking ahead, and using coupons. She had always lived this way; Rebekah's mom had taught her to use coupons and to buy groceries on sale. Learning from her turned out to be just the beginning of my adventure in savings!

I ran with my newfound knowledge. It's amazing how little you can spend when you are focused. Over the next few months, I learned many creative ways to save money. In one year's time, I was pleased to see our grocery and dining-out budget go from $1,100 per month to under $200 per month!

Thrilled, I shared my savings success story with friends. Soon, I was teaching savvy saving ideas to other people who wanted to learn too. I taught my first class to thirty women in a friend's home. From there, I began to teach classes in her home every month. Often, the workshops were in such high demand that there wasn't enough space to admit everyone who was interested.

This led to the successful launch of the Faithful Provisions blog (www.Faithful Provisions.com) and an e-mail subscription with daily money-saving tips. Local and national media followed as thousands discovered that they, too, could slash their grocery bills and save money.

What I soon learned was that this was part of God's plan for me and just the beginning of my opportunity to trust in Him. In the winter of 2009, the economic downturn that had been affecting families across the country finally impacted us. My husband's job was downsized, and he found himself unemployed with a wife, two children, a mortgage, and bills. His salary, bonus, car, fuel card, and benefits like healthcare were all gone. I had left my job voluntarily and now my husband was laid off—what a turn of events from four years before!

As a wife and mother, it is difficult to see your husband struggle with the double whammy of losing his job and the loss of income that comes with it. Sure, Bradford's ego was bruised, but he had peace with the circumstances. No sooner than the day after the layoff, God opened the door for me to teach more classes. This time, however, churches were calling to schedule workshops, and they actually wanted to pay me to do it!

Bradford knew restoring his career was going to be a challenge in this new economy, but he set about trying to find a job. The offers didn't pour in, so it was during this period that he took a deeper interest in the Faithful Provisions blog. I was pleased when he approached me about offering to help out with sales and business planning. A dream of mine was coming true. I had always wanted to work from home with my husband, doing something we enjoyed. After all, he is my best friend! Since then, he has gone back to work outside the home, but we continue to work together on growing our business.

With the money-saving strategies we learned in the time leading up to the layoff, we were in a position not only to stretch our budget, but to help others do the same and encourage generosity in those who were struggling.

My hope is that in sharing our journey, you will be encouraged to see God's promises fulfilled in the practical realm as well as the spiritual. As you step out in faith, I believe that God will help you just like He helped us.

Are you ready to begin your saving savvy adventure?

Chapter 1

SAVE MONEY, LIVE GENEROUSLY

What if you could save 50 percent or more on your grocery bill without giving up the things you love? What other things would you spend your money on if you could cut your grocery bill in half? Would you like to save money on every purchase you make? In what ways could you be generous and help others with the money you are saving?

If you like to save money, you are in the right place! I love to get bargains on the things I need, and now I have more control over that than ever before.

Why do I want to save money? It allows my family to do things that we wouldn't normally do. It provides us an opportunity to make purchases without going into debt and to go places we might otherwise never venture. The savings we realize from being savvy shoppers allow us to save money for the future—for items we plan to buy or to put into savings, a retirement account, or our kids' college accounts.

. . . .

Those who have been given a trust must prove faithful.

1 CORINTHIANS 4:2

. . . .

Another benefit from shopping wisely is that it gives us the ability to share generously with others. Because we aren't spending as much money on groceries, we can give joyfully to others. Not out of obligation or duty, but because we have such abundance and it is fun to bless others out of what we have been entrusted with. We give away more now than we did as a dual-income family with no children. My, how our priorities have shifted! We are able to give our time, talents, money, food, and other donations on a regular basis . . . all because we save on our everyday spending.

. . . .

Remember this: Whoever sows sparingly will also reap sparingly,

and whoever sows generously will also reap generously.

2 CORINTHIANS 9:6

. . . .

Your circumstances may differ from ours:

- ◇ You may be trying to get out of debt and need to find another way to save.
- ◇ You may be saving up to make a big purchase like a car or a home.
- ◇ You may be trying to find extra money to put toward your mortgage, college savings, or retirement.
- ◇ You may just be trying to put food on the table and make ends meet.

No matter what your circumstance, you can learn how to get control of your spending and start saving money today, and I will show you how.

Do You Want to Save More?

Times are difficult in our country. Families are facing tough decisions in their everyday lives. Just go online or open a magazine or newspaper, and you will be confronted by all that is plaguing families:

- ◇ Underemployment is high.[1]
- ◇ Average incomes are flat.[2]

- Food and gas prices are rising.[3]
- The savings rate is at its lowest in US history.[4]

And yet, while all of that is happening, we are also seeing:

- A rise in volunteer activity.[5]
- Declines in consumer-credit-card use.[6]
- The highest rate of coupon redemption in years.[7]

Many families are in saving and maintaining mode right now. They are going without or seeking less expensive options. They are paying attention to the price of fuel and the price of milk. They have shopped their insurance and refinanced their mortgage.

What else can families or individuals do to save money? That is where I can help. In this book, I will:

- show you how to avoid paying full price for items you use every day
- teach you practical ways to trim your grocery budget while keeping your pantry stocked
- encourage you to reconsider how you shop for groceries
- explain how to have plenty left over to share with others

Saving Savvy provides common-sense solutions that will help you stretch your dollars, purchase strategically, and give away more than you ever dreamed possible. My goal is to introduce you to the many practical tools and resources available that will help you save money.

What Is Saving Savvy?

According to Dictionary.com, the word *savvy* means to be experienced, shrewd, and informed; to know.[8] In short, I want you to be shrewd and informed shoppers who make the smartest purchasing decisions possible. If your goal is to save money, then utilize the tools in this book that will help you work smarter, not harder. Once you learn how to be savvy in your saving, you will spend less time trying to save money and have more time to spend with the people you love. You will have money for the things you need and give away more than you ever thought you could.

Does This Really Work?

Some of you might be wondering, *Does this really work?* or, *Can I even do this?* The answer lies in how badly you want to make a change. The resources and tools in this book do work, and yes, you can do it! The level at which you implement these tools will depend on your available time. Those who have more time to commit will save more, and those who have less time will save but maybe not on as large a scale.

The reasons people turn to strategic saving and couponing are many.

Some see it as an income. Jennifer says, "I think of coupons as free cash. I don't throw away money, so thinking of coupons as cash helps me to keep on going and to stay committed. And now that I have no job, it makes couponing even more important to my family."

Some make it into a game. Christina was thrilled when her receipt said she had saved $68. "I only spent $20! I feel like it was payday when I went shopping . . . it's a game and a challenge."

Some had money-saving strategies engrained in them. Ann explains, "I grew up cutting and sorting coupons. My mom, aunts, and grandmother all do it."

Some see it as God's provision. Brandi is grateful for the savings strategies she put into place several months ago. "I have a four-year-old son and my mother-in-law lives with me. I think God brought me to couponing because He realized I would need it in the future. My husband was killed in a car accident three months ago. God, friends, and family have gotten me through it emotionally, and couponing has helped me tremendously."

LIVING *Generously* TIP

A benefit of shopping wisely is that it gives you the ability to share generously with others.

. . . .

He has given food and provision to those who
reverently and worshipfully fear Him.

PSALM 111:5 AMP

. . . .

Your reasons for becoming a savvy shopper may be the same as some of our readers or totally different. No matter the reason, everyone likes to save money.

What Are Your Goals?

My goals initially were to save money, to be a better manager of our family's finances, and to find ways to give. What do you want to accomplish? Do you want to make your budget stretch further? Learn how to use coupons? Figure out how to stock up on the foods your family eats? No matter what your motivations, the process begins with setting goals.

Here are a few tips to help you define and nurture your goals:

Write them down. A goal not written down is just a dream. Writing down your finalized list of goals will give you focus. Put them where you will see them every day.

Weed your list of goals. Your initial list of goals may be large. Rather than take them all on, give some time and consideration to them, and, like pulling weeds from the garden, narrow your list down to the most important ones. The more specific the list, the better.

Surround yourself with like-minded people. If your goal is to save money and time and to be wiser in your shopping, seek out those who do it well and find forums where you can share ideas and ask questions. Find a group of friends to read this book with you and encourage each other as you put these strategies into practice. Build a team of people around you who have similar goals and understand your point of view.

A Paradigm Shift: Never Pay Full Price Again

The most important thing about saving money with the methods and resources outlined in the upcoming pages is to change the way you think about shopping. The way we are going to approach saving will be a paradigm shift in how you view your everyday purchases. The ultimate goal is never to pay full price again.

SAVING SAVVY TIP

Your ultimate goal for your everyday purchases is never to pay full price again.

Think about it this way. Instead of running out and purchasing what you need right now at whatever price it is on the shelf, you will only purchase items that are a good deal. As you incorporate this savvy saving lifestyle, you will find that almost everything you need, you have on hand. You purchased those items during previous sales, and hopefully at least half off the retail price. All you are doing now is seeking great deals on the items you will need in the future. Because you are planning ahead, you have fewer financial "emergencies." You reduce the amount you spend on unexpected purchases when you don't *have* to make a big grocery purchase every week.

What Is Your Shopping Comfort Zone?

Getting out of your shopping comfort zone can be hard, and the change may seem overwhelming at first. Whenever you are doing something new, you will have lots of questions. Also, as you begin to implement these savvy saving strategies, you might feel like you are swimming against the current. But if you stick with it, you'll be amazed at how much more money you'll have at the end of every month.

Consider for a moment anyone who has achieved greatness in a chosen field. How did they become so great? They didn't roll out of bed one morning and decide to be the greatest at what they do.

- They put in time to hone their skills.
- They have a coach, a mentor, or a trusted adviser to help them navigate the journey.
- They view setbacks as opportunities to improve.
- They have clearly defined goals.
- They have a positive attitude.
- They act on their God-given talent.

You might be wondering what this has to do with saving money. Plenty. You have recognized something you want to change (save money), and now you have a goal in mind. You have a coach who will help you reach your goal (*Saving Savvy* and FaithfulProvisions .com). You may meet with some resistance on this path to savings, but with time and practice, you will overcome that. By reading this book, you will learn how to save money and live generously. You are taking the positive action necessary to reach your goals.

There is an old saying about learning to walk before you can run, and that is true for savvy saving as well. If you have never shopped sale items, used coupons, stocked ahead, or planned meals, how can you be expected to know what to do? As you read the following chapters, keep these two points in mind:

1. *Take your time.* This is a marathon, not a sprint.
2. *Allow yourself some grace.* We all mess up sometimes.

A Time to Learn

Before you read further, take a moment to answer the following questions. They will help you decide where you are going to spend your time in this book.

1. When you hear the term *stocking up*, what comes to mind?

    a. Wow, my pantry is empty.

    b. I have some food and other items on hand.

c. My food is organized, I didn't pay full price, and I have peace of mind.

d. Armageddon.

___ 2. How much time do you put into planning visits to the grocery store?

a. Not much.

b. Some.

c. I put in enough time to be prepared to take advantage of sales.

d. I don't have time to plan.

___ 3. What best describes the contents of your freezer?

a. Full of UFOs (unidentified frozen objects).

b. Clean but complicated—many kinds of containers with contents dated a year ago!

c. Clean and uncomplicated—clearly labeled containers with dates.

d. Really, really cold food.

___ 4. How often do you make a meal plan?

a. Never, but I'd like to try.

b. Sometimes, but it is not a habit.

c. Often, because it is the best way to save money.

d. I don't plan meals; I eat them.

___ 5. How often do you use coupons for grocery items?

a. Not often, because I can't keep track of them and don't think I save that much.

b. Sometimes, but I never seem to have them with me.

c. Often. I add coupons to sale items for deeper savings.

d. What are coupons?

_c_ 6. How organized are you when you visit the grocery store to shop?

    a. Unorganized, but I want to get better.

    b. Somewhat organized, but I need a little help.

    c. Highly organized—and I know the specific aisles to visit.

    d. I left my shopping list on the kitchen counter next to my phone.

_b_ 7. How generous are you?

    a. I want to give, but financially we can't right now.

    b. I give some, but I could give more.

    c. I give items and time on a regular basis.

    d. Thanks, but I gave at the office.

If you answered . . .

mostly "a": You are an open canvas. Get ready—you will be learning more than you ever dreamed possible. This will be such a fun and fruitful journey for you. Your life will never be the same, and neither will your wallet!

mostly "b": You have begun your journey to saving, but there are many new and wonderful tips to unveil. Since you have already dabbled in saving, you are clearly eager to learn more—and it is all about the attitude.

mostly "c": The biggest job for you is to fine-tune your already-learned skills. Find tips and tools that will not only help you save more money, but save you more time.

mostly "d": We have a little work to do. But don't worry! You are reading this book, and that means you have the attitude and the interest to do what it takes to turn your spending around.

Depending on how you answered, you are demonstrating that you may have much to learn or already know more than you think. To some, this is a whole new way to provide for their family. Others have been doing some of these things for a while but want to take their savings knowledge a step further and begin to live generously. No matter where you are, this book will provide you with more ways to save.

. . . .

God loves a cheerful giver.

2 CORINTHIANS 9:7

. . . .

How Much Time Can You Invest?

In the coming chapters, you will be presented with many options to save money. Each will have pros and cons. You will choose which savings strategies to implement according to what interests you or what fits your particular season of life. But ultimately, the tools and resources you choose will be determined by how much time you have to devote to them.

For those who have more time for things like meal planning, shopping to stock up, and couponing, your savings will stack up much more quickly. Still, even with less time, you can save money by selecting a few strategies in this book and incorporating them.

For instance, as we will describe in detail later, meal planning can save you quite a bit on your grocery budget. However, if you aren't good at planning, or if you don't have the time to make weekly meal plans, what can you do? You may choose to invest in a meal-planning service to do the work for you. You can then use other savings strategies, such as stocking up or couponing, to counteract the costs incurred by subscribing to a meal-planning service. You'll still be saving money; you'll just be adapting these strategies to what works best for you and your family.

As you read, consider each tool presented in the book and the amount of time it will take you to implement. Everyone is different, so the savvy saving ideas you put to use will be different from those that someone else chooses. Simply choose what works best for you.

This book isn't about implementing every single strategy. It's about choosing a path to savvy saving that works for you.

Getting Your Family on Board

Before you even start your savvy saving lifestyle, you must get your family on board in some capacity. You know your family best, so consider what motivates them and use that to get their help in maintaining this new way of living.

Saving for a Family Trip or Event

Encourage one another to seek out sales and coupons or to go without "wants" in order to save up for a fun family vacation or event such as a Disney trip. Make your goals specific and measurable so you can see your progress.

> " *A great way to visualize your savings is to add up the amount of money from your receipts that you saved by couponing and put that money in a big glass jar on your counter. (You could use Monopoly money to make it fun.) Tell your family that when you get to a certain amount, you'll use the savings for a family event or purchase. Have them help decide the goal.* "
>
> —Joan

Keeping Their Favorite Foods Stocked

Those of you with teenagers, or boys for that matter, know how hard it is to keep food stocked when it's going out faster than you can get it on the shelf. Why not use "Inventory Lists" (see chapter 3) and encourage your husband and teenagers to cross off items they've eaten? This way you can always keep their favorite foods on hand.

> *My husband was not on board the first year. He thought it was a waste of time and didn't see the true savings. So in January of the second year I challenged him to match dollar-for-dollar all my coupon savings. I would save my receipts, and in December he would write me a check for that amount. December came, and let's just say he was convinced when he ended up writing a check for over $1,200.*
>
> —Latasha

Teach Your Children about Money

In addition to saving money yourself, you can teach your children the value of money at an early age. Getting the whole family involved on grocery trips is not only fun (if you have the trip well-planned) but is a great way to instill your values in a very practical way. The best way to learn is by experience, and what better experience than to give your children some ownership and responsibilities with the family grocery budget? Not only are you teaching them how to save money, but you are helping them with lifelong skills like math, decision making, and problem solving.

> *My kids are ten and seven, and when we go to the store, they each get a stack of coupons that they are in charge of. They find the item, load it in the cart, and figure out how much the item will cost after sales, store coupons,*

and manufacturer coupons. One thing they like is when we have a coupon for an item that they really want, we can sometimes get it because it will be so cheap. **„**

—Emily

What You Will Learn in This Book

In the coming chapters, I will help you get started by focusing on the things you need to do to save. I will give you saving savvy tips about:

◇ *Stocking up*—making room for the items you will purchase cheaply

◇ *Using your freezer*—how to preserve meats and produce properly

◇ *Meal planning*—easy steps to plan your weekly dishes

◇ *Using coupons*—tips for using coupons with sale items to get deeper savings

◇ *Planning your grocery trip*—learning to plan before you shop

◇ *Going to the grocery store*—shopping wisely to maximize your savings

◇ *Living generously*—using the money you save to benefit others

The following chapters will show you how to implement the resources and tools we discuss. You will then determine what fits you and your season of life. So let's get started!

INTERACTIVE RESOURCES

Throughout this book you will find symbols like the one here. These are two-dimensional barcodes that can store link, plain text, SMS

Faithful Provisions Facebook Page

text message, addresses, URLs, Geo location, e-mail, phone numbers, and contact information. They are used for quick connections (response) between static and online content. The easiest way to describe them is as paper-based hyperlinks. Once you have downloaded a compatible QR Code Scan Reader (we recommend the Scanlife or Mobio App), take a picture of the code using your phone camera, and you will be linked to the related information.

You can access this book's website at www.savingsavvybook.com.

Faithful Provisions Free E-mail Newsletter

Use your phone's camera to take a picture of the QR codes to the left to visit the official Facebook page for Faithful Provisions or to sign up for free e-mail updates from Faithful Provisions.com.

Chapter 2

....

STOCKING UP

This chapter will help you prepare your pantry for items you will stock up on at a discounted price. (I will cover specific strategies for saving money later.) Now, to be fair, getting your kitchen ready is not a glamorous part of the savings process. It is going to take a little work and thought so you can maximize your space.

The blessing of preparing your pantry—and it will be a big blessing for you and your family—is that you will:

- ◇ Be ready to take advantage of good deals because you have a place to stock up.
- ◇ Save your sanity by knowing what you have on hand and what you need.
- ◇ Save time through organization and knowing where things are.
- ◇ Save money because you will buy things at the best price.
- ◇ Be more generous because you will have surplus to give.

> *It's nice to have stuff that I know I can put together to make a great meal and not have to run to the store. Now I plan my meals based on what's in the pantry. It's so simple, and we've already been able to tell a difference in our bank account!*
>
> —*Melanie*

A Generation Removed

Mama Kelly was my grandmother, who I am named after. I spent a lot of time with her while I was growing up, and every visit included a table laden with her homemade fare: fried chicken, mashed potatoes, plus tomatoes and green beans fresh from the garden. As a bedtime snack we would crumble pieces of dinner's leftover cornbread into a tall glass of thick, whole milk. When my sisters and I spent the night, we enjoyed her homemade chocolate gravy and biscuits for breakfast! These fond food memories remain some of my favorite indulgences today.

As I began to put into practice my new lifestyle of saving, I realized that Mama Kelly was a master of preparing her pantry and stocking up. Most people are completely unaware that past generations lived this way, but as a mom today, I think my grandmother's generation had it right.

Mama Kelly kept a storeroom, and its shelving ran the length of the room. A flowery-patterned, homespun curtain hung over the shelves, which were stocked with my grandmother's canning. She had a huge garden, and its harvest packed the storeroom full of creamed corn, stewed tomatoes, canned green beans, preserves, and pickles, just to name a few! Always darkened to keep the sun from spoiling her canned goods, this room was a quiet retreat on a hot summer day. I still remember how cool the linoleum floors felt under my bare feet. The storeroom was a testimony to my mother's childhood, growing up on a farm in the Delta, where stocking ahead was a way of life.

This wasn't the only fully stocked storage area Mama Kelly kept. Her chest freezer was full of vegetables, homemade jams, and meats. One of my favorite things about our visits was leaving with a load of her homemade strawberry and peach freezer jams and her spicy canned pickles. This is where I got my love for cooking, because I can't buy anything like that in a store today. At Mama Kelly's, everything was made from scratch.

Now, I am not suggesting that everyone run out and start a garden or cook from scratch. You may not have the space or the time to do this. What I am saying is that if you slow down, take stock of what you have, use your space a little better, and decide what is important to your family, you can make your money go farther.

Organizing the Pantry

In many homes, the kitchen is a high-traffic area. Because of that, your pantry needs to be organized before you begin stocking up, so you'll know where things are. Organizing your pantry (or kitchen cabinets, or wherever you store food) obviously isn't a necessity for saving money, but if you have time, it helps to make space for all those extra items you will find on sale.

When you clean out your pantry, have a large box in the kitchen where you can easily place usable items to be donated to a food pantry or charity organization.

The first step is to take everything out of your pantry (or food storage area). This will give you the chance not only to sweep it out and clean the shelves, but also to find usable items you can donate or expired items you can discard.

Next, organize the items in a way that makes sense to you. Here are a few guide-lines to keep in mind as you organize your pantry:

- ◇ Put heavy items on the floor.
- ◇ Place lighter-weight and less-used items toward the top.
- ◇ Put glass jars and breakable items out of the reach of young children.
- ◇ Organize items by expiration date—put the earliest-expiring items in front.

Making Space

A challenge many people have when they begin to stock up is a lack of storage space. Since you will be getting multiples of great deals, you need somewhere to put them all—somewhere you won't forget about them! To solve this problem, you just have to be creative.

> " *I cleared a linen closet by only keeping two sheet sets for each bed. One stays on the bed, and the second set is stored under the mattress, which is right where you need it. Also, you only need two towels per person. Hang these on door hooks [to clear additional space in the linen closet].* "
>
> —*Leanna*

LIVING Generously TIP

Place a "donation" box in the garage to capture all your extra items in one place.

For food items, my husband added extra wire shelving (purchased inexpensively at a home improvement store) to the top and bottom of my pantry where previously there had been wasted space. This enables me to better group the items we use the most and store more food in our kitchen, as opposed to somewhere else.

Our "somewhere else" is a designated area in the garage. There, we utilize two metal storage lockers that my husband had used in his previous job and were no longer needed. They perfectly meet our needs because they allow us to stock and store our nonperishable items in a cabinet behind a secure door.

Here are a few tips I have learned about storing food in the garage over the years:

◊ If you are storing nonperishable food items, make sure they are in a secured cabinet to deter unwanted pests.

◊ You can get metal storage cabinets at any office supply store.

- Make sure young children know this space is off-limits. That unopened box of cheese crackers may look very appealing to a hungry preschooler.
- If you want to be more creative, go to a storage facility and see if they have any shelves that have been left behind by previous renters. They usually throw them away.

For nonperishable items like paper towels and cleaning products, my husband added extra shelving in the garage. Again, make sure young children know this is an off-limits area. In the search for space, we found a usable place in the laundry room above the cabinets. For us, this is an ideal spot for storing items that may need climate control. Also, we keep additional fabric softener and detergent there. A plastic storage container that slides under your bed is a great place for your stash of toiletries.

> " *Each stockpile item I buy has a clear plastic storage tub. I try not to buy more than that tub will hold unless it is a super deal or something that does not go on sale often.* "
>
> —Kenzi

Determine What You Already Have

Although my stocking-up strategies will focus on the grocery store, the process really begins at home—specifically in your pantry, freezer, and refrigerator. The first question a financial counselor asks someone trying to live on a budget is, "Do you know how much money you have?" Similarly, as your "kitchen counselor," I want you to know how much food you have! Before you begin to implement the savvy saving strategies in this book, you need to properly assess the food you already have on hand. Again, this step isn't a necessity, but it will help in storage and planning.

Know Your Family's Staple Items

If you're unclear about what foods would be considered staples, Karen Ehman, author of *The Complete Guide to Getting and Staying Organized*, explains that staples—like flour, sugar, and salt—are where you start when you want to make something. She writes, "From staples you can make an array of entrees, side dishes, and desserts. 'Who has the time?' you ask. I've found that when I say that, what I really mean is, 'I don't want to make the time.'

"If a friend calls and wants to chat," says Karen, "do you stop and talk for twenty minutes or so? That's about how long it takes to whip up a batch of homemade muffins, cookies, or granola. We greatly overestimate how long it takes to cook from scratch. And in this case, time is money. We can reduce our grocery bills if we begin to cook and bake rather than buying ready-made foods. The transition won't happen overnight, but you can begin now to make small changes toward being a more frugal shopper and cook."[1]

As you find out what you have on hand, you will begin to notice (if you have not already) what your family's staple items are. Make a list of these items: they are the ones you eat the most of. The following sample list shows some common staple items, though yours may vary. Perhaps you are vegetarian, on a gluten-free or sugar-free diet, or are watching your weight. Whatever your diet or family situation, the items you buy most often might differ greatly from mine, which means your grocery budget is not going to be the same. I keep my staples list in a small spiral notebook and carry it in my shopping tote so it's always with me.

COMMON FOOD STAPLES

PANTRY	Canned Tomatoes	Chicken Broth	Pastas	Cereals	Snacks
	Canned Vegetables	Beans	Taco Shells	Rice/ Grains	Peanut Butter
	Flour	Sugar	Salt	Cocoa	Condi- ments
FREEZER	Meats	Cheese	Vegetables	Pizza	Casseroles
REFRIGERA- TOR	Milk/ Eggs	Yogurt	Sour Cream	Tortillas	Biscuits/ Dough

When you shop for common staples like packaged cheese, yogurt, butter, tortillas, and sour cream, be sure to look for the items with the latest expiration date. Grocery stores stock the shelves with fresher items toward the back. These types of products can have a two- to three-month shelf life prior to opening. So I can purchase six tubs of sour cream for half price (or free if I have a good coupon!) and get enough to last a month or two if I remember to check the expiration dates and plan my meals with this ingredient.

To maximize your savings, be flexible and try off-brand or store-brand products.

Once you have determined what you have on hand and what your staples are, it's time to go shopping, right? Not just yet. You'll need to have the space to store the items you are stocking up on.

In our family, there are a few favorite items that we purchase no matter the price (within reason). One of the best ways to use your stockpile is to stock up on your family's favorites when they are on sale.

This is especially pertinent when you are brand loyal to a certain product. It is okay to be brand loyal on a few items, just not all! So if your family prefers a certain kind of toilet paper, you better stock up when it goes on sale. Once you start watching the sales cycles, you will learn how *much* you need to stock up according to the frequency of the sale and the quantity of product your family uses.

Try not to be brand loyal on everything. Typically, name-brand products cost more than off-brand or store brands. If your goal is saving money at the grocery store, then decide now what you and your family will be flexible on.

Use a Price List to Know Good Prices

So what is a good price? This was one of the first things I realized I didn't know and that I needed to know. Talk about a learning curve! I quickly found out I was not equipped to purchase my staple items strategically, because I didn't know what a good price was. So knowing a good price on the items you purchase is key to saving money.

Provisions Price List
Download

If you are low on time, one of the smartest tools you can take advantage of is a price list. Even if you don't have time to shop multiple stores, use coupons, or stock up, you can download a price list app (such as my free Provisions Price List app for iPhone) on your smartphone or print a document outlining good prices (the free Provisions Price List at FaithfulProvisions.com). Equip yourself with these tools to make your life easier. No guesswork needed.

A price list is an index of a good purchase price for any item. For instance, last week a local grocery store advertised boneless, skinless chicken breasts on sale for $3.99/pound. If I was new to savvy shopping, I would assume that is a good price since it is on "sale" and featured in the store ad. But if I pulled out my handy-dandy Provisions Price List, I would know that the best price is $1.99/pound. That is a big difference. The good news is, I didn't need to do a lot of work to gain that knowledge; I just needed to use the free resources available to me.

> " *I save at least 30 percent every time I go to the store, and sometimes as much as 60 percent. I can now walk into a store and see that sometimes their "lowest prices" are not the lowest, especially if I wait for an item to go on sale when I can use a coupon. The old saying that "knowledge is power" is definitely true—especially when stretching your grocery dollars!* "
>
> *—Angela*

Stocking Up

Stocking up on items when they are at their lowest price has proven to be one of the best ways to decrease overall grocery spending. Remember, your shopping goal is never to pay full price! Here's how stocking up should flow:

- ◇ Figure out what you have on hand and what your grocery staples are.
- ◇ Know what a good sale price is—be educated!
- ◇ Determine how much room you have for storage.
- ◇ Purchase your staple items when they are on sale—often half price or less.
- ◇ Buy enough of the product to get you through until it goes on sale again.
- ◇ Look for ways to give to others from what you have on hand.
- ◇ And never, never pay full price!

When I first started to stock up on great deals, I learned that in order to build my reserves, I needed to plan ahead. This is true for everyone. If you go to the grocery store without a plan, you will just buy random things. You might score some bargains, but you will not be making the most of your money or your time. In fact, you will probably end up spending an hour or two and come home with a hodgepodge of items, and have to return to the store later.

Where Do I Begin?

Let's answer the question you are likely asking yourself right now: *Where do I begin?* The answer is right there in your kitchen.

> " *Stocking up was a new concept to me. I learned that if you buy several of an item when you find a good deal, then you will never have to pay full price for that item again. I started with buying one extra item a week and built up from there. Eventually I noticed that my spending was going down, but we had more and more food in the house.* "
>
> —*Staci*

When you find a good deal, purchase extras to donate to local charities, food banks, and homeless shelters.

A well-stocked pantry saves you money because, with your staples on hand, you won't have to make a last-minute trip to the grocery store. I don't know about you, but I never get just one thing at the grocery store. If I have to go to all the trouble of getting out and making a trip, I want to feel like I have accomplished more than grabbing one measly tub of sour cream! Without a plan, I usually end up picking up all kinds of impulse buys that I don't need and spending way too much. An unplanned trip to the grocery store typically exceeds my grocery budget by 50 percent or more, and I suspect the same is true for you.

Many shoppers think of warehouse and wholesale clubs when they think of buying in bulk. But you don't have to be a member of a club to buy in bulk. Bulk buying is something you can do at your local grocery store on a weekly basis. For example, when your grocery is running a "10 for $10" sale on toothpaste, meaning it is only $1 per tube, then buy ten tubes! Sure, that's ten extra dollars you're spending that week, but what a deal! This is much better than buying toothpaste one at a time, when it is at regular price, and paying $3 per tube. You may ask, "Do I need all this toothpaste?" In my house the answer is no, so we keep what we need and donate the rest to others.

The key to successful stockpiling is organization. But don't groan if you aren't organized! There are multiple tools and resources available to help you get and stay organized. My goal is to make the process of saving easy for you, not more complicated.

Thinking Ahead

You now have an understanding of what you need, what you have on hand, and what your staple items are. And hopefully you have organized your pantry and storage areas, so you have space for your stockpiled items.

As you begin to fill in your stockpile, you need to think ahead. The seasons play a major role in what goes on sale and what foods are in abundance. For instance, if you want to serve pork tenderloin for Christmas dinner, you need to think about finding it on sale as early as October. That way you aren't caught the week before Christmas paying full price for something you could have gotten at a fraction of the cost by planning ahead.

As Thanksgiving approaches, most baking items go on sale; so in early October I start stocking up on sale-priced sugar, flour, oil, canned pumpkin, and even icing. This helps me when birthdays come around, because I already have all the ingredients to make a great birthday cake—at less than half the price. Or, as summer hits, you will find an abundance of marinades, salad dressings, and grilling meats at deep discounts. This is a great time to really stock up, since many of these items only rarely hit that deep discount during the year.

. . . .

And [God] Who provides seed for the sower and bread for
eating will also provide and multiply your [resources for]
sowing and increase the fruits of your righteousness [which
manifests itself in active goodness, kindness, and charity].

2 CORINTHIANS 9:10 AMP

. . . .

Benefits of Stocking Up

Remember, stocking up when items are on sale means you never have to pay full price. You're saving money, and as stocking up becomes your habit, you'll find it will save loads of precious time!

In addition to saving money, stocking up has some unexpected benefits:

Peace

I can relax, knowing that my staples are on hand and available. Like having money in the bank, I feel good, and things just seem to go more smoothly when I am stocked up and prepared. After all, I don't have thirty minutes to throw away, and I bet you don't either.

Meal Preparation

I can feel good about the fact that I am able to prepare wholesome and healthy meals for my family. Honestly, when I am really hungry and there's nothing in the fridge, pantry, or freezer, I will be the first person to order pizza or go out for Mexican food! Nothing against those delicious foods, but a typical restaurant meal is not as nutritious—or as affordable—as homemade. When you cook, you control the salt, sugar, and fat content. You know how clean your kitchen is, as well as the hands that prepared the food.

Save your dining-out money for special occasions, and focus on making your kitchen the place your family prefers.

Family Time at the Table

These days, many families struggle to have family meals together. But by having a well-stocked pantry, you can create some uninterrupted family time around your kitchen table. What's more, you'll create memories that last forever. You know all those conversations you've been trying to have with your kids, or the need you've felt to connect with your spouse about what is important to him? The dinner table is a perfect time and place to create a loving, trusting atmosphere for open communication. In many cultures, the dinner table is cherished and seen as a place to connect. Bring that experience to your family by keeping your pantry stocked, making you ready for family bonding opportunities.

Food for Others

Because I'm stocked up, I can give away food to others. I've found that having a full pantry makes this so easy to do. There is no rushing around to buy extra food, because you already have it on hand. Homemade meals can be a real ministry to folks who are experiencing difficulties such as the loss of a loved one or a stressful time at work. A home-cooked meal can also be the perfect gift for a new mom. When I have

LIVING *Generously* TIP

As you stock up on groceries, look for opportunities to bless others with home-cooked meals.

an abundance of food, I cheerfully give out of my surplus! Then it is both easy and enjoyable for me to pull together a nutritious and delicious meal for someone else.

Getting control of your pantry is an important first step in the saving savvy lifestyle. Now that you know what you have on hand, what you need to stock up on, and you have the space to store things, generosity will flow from your pantry.

. . . .

The wise store up choice food and olive oil.

PROVERBS 21:20

. . . .

Know When to Stop

When it comes to stocking up, my rule of thumb is that you stop stocking up each week when you run out of money. The quantity of individual items you purchase is going to be different for everyone, because we all have different household needs. Getting specialty items like gluten-free or sugar-free products on sale may be important for you. If you have young children, you could stockpile diapers continually; there is always a brand of diapers on sale. And at the other end of the spectrum, if you have teenagers with insatiable appetites, then your stash of snack items may never stay full, regardless of your efforts. However, this is one concept that stays the same no matter your situation: when the money is gone, you are done!

> *We didn't think we could live on a cash-only basis. We started out by moving the grocery and household goods category in our budget to cash-only. It has amazed us both how much living cash-only in these areas has helped us stay on track with our budget. We not only stay on track, but we even spend less because we are aware of every penny. Once the envelope is empty, that's it until the next week.*
>
> —*Sally*

SAVINGS STRATEGIES FOR
PREPARING YOUR PANTRY

. . . .

IF YOU HAVE *MORE* TIME . . .

1. **Make space and organize.** Clean out and organize your pantry.

2. **Know your staple items.** Create a list of all your most frequently purchased items.

3. **Buy seasonally.** Think ahead and plan to purchase seasonal items.

. . . .

IF YOU HAVE *LESS* TIME . . .

1. **Use a price list.** Print out or download the Provisions Price List from Faith fulProvisions.com to reference when you are shopping.

2. **Start stocking up.** When your favorite items go on sale, buy extras so you never pay full price.

Chapter 3

....

WARMING UP TO
THE FREEZER

Did you know that your freezer can be one of your best tools for saving money? That's right. The cold, hard fact is that this appliance can help bring your food costs down like nothing else. By learning how to properly freeze your wisely purchased food for later, the work that you put into the freezer will be more than worthwhile. Once you have a plan for your freezer (just like the pantry), you will be able to shop smart, stock up on your favorite foods, and save money.

> " *I buy ground beef when it's really on sale and then have a big cooking day,*
> *making and freezing every meal I can think of that uses ground beef (lasa-*
> *gna, meatballs, burger patties, etc.). It saves lots of money, and I love being*
> *able to pull out a meal that's ready to go on a busy night!* "
>
> —Heather

I was amazed at how I could make use of my freezer to save money, just by implementing a few easy tasks. As we've seen, my main goal is never to pay full price, and my freezer helps me accomplish that.

There are three broad steps to take in approaching the use of your freezer:

Step 1: Clean

Step 2: Organize

Step 3: Invest

It's difficult to know what to do until you know what you have to work with, so let's start with cleaning. This is simple: clean out the freezer and get rid of what you don't recognize, need, or eat. The next step is to organize. Now that you have this cleaned-up space, I'll show you how you can best use it. Finally, if you are able, invest in a stand-alone freezer. For most people, the freezer that came with your refrigerator won't have the capacity for stocking up in a big way. If you decide you want to stock up, then acquiring more freezer space will open you up for advanced techniques that take a little time and money but will help maximize your savings.

So, if you are ready, put on your mittens and let's go together into the space where time froze: the freezer.

Step 1: Clean

Keep a box of baking soda in the freezer to prevent any smells from contaminating your foods.

Whether our freezers are stand-alone or part of our refrigerator, we don't really know what is in there. To be able to properly store all the food you didn't pay full price for, like chicken breasts or ground beef, you're going to need to prepare some space. Again, since most people do not spend time in the freezer, chances are it will be in need of some attention. You know that box of frozen waffles with an inch of ice in the far depths of the back of your freezer, or that half-used bag of peas that have shriveled and are no longer edible? Time to get rid of them. Take back that space and use it for food you will actually eat.

The following simple but helpful steps are designed to motivate and encourage you as you prepare to stock up on those sale items.

Create Room

Have you pulled something from the freezer and wondered what in the world it was? I call these UFOs—Unidentified Frozen Objects. If you don't remember the last time you cleaned out your freezer, there is no time like the present! You'll be surprised at what you don't recognize and how disorganized it is in there. Among the unrecognizable casseroles and meats, I've heard of people finding long-forgotten wedding cake, exploded soft drinks, even a baby shark caught on a family vacation. One homeschooling mom I know found the bug collection her son had gathered years before as a science project. Hmm . . . time to clean it out, girl! After you have removed the mystery items, place the things you want to keep in a cooler.

Clean and Defrost

Refer to the manufacturer's instructions on how to clean and defrost your freezer unit. Once you have done that, wipe it down, inside and out, with a solution of water and white vinegar. Vinegar will help remove odors and cuts through grease and stains. Sprinkle some salt or baking soda to make an abrasive to remove tough stains.

VINEGAR CLEANING SOLUTION

Here is a great recipe for a cleaning solution you can make at home. It is inexpensive and can be used to clean just about anything. If you don't like the smell of vinegar, add some essential oils in a scent you prefer.

1 cup water
1 cup vinegar
1–3 drops essential oils (optional)

Combine in a spray bottle and store for all your cleaning needs.

Purge Unneeded Items

As part of your cleaning process (and preferably on a regular basis thereafter), check expiration dates on everything. I find that items like bread and vegetables don't do well after two to three months in the freezer, no matter how you package them. Freezer burn tends to get to these foods quickly, so I try to stay aware and rotate them frequently. Meats, on the other hand, will keep longer in the freezer without compromising texture or consistency. More than once I have pulled out a cut of meat that has been frozen for a year and it still tasted great!

Here is a guideline for the freezer life of some common food items you can stock ahead:

FREEZER LIFE FOR COMMON FOODS

FOOD ITEM	FREEZER LIFE MONTHS
SOUPS/BROTHS	6-8
BEEF	6-12
CHICKEN	6-12
PORK	4-6
FISH	3-6
BERRIES	6
BREADS	2-3
GREEN BEANS	10
TOMATOES	10

*Note: I find that fish is the most difficult item to make taste good from frozen.

Here is a guideline for freezer life of some less common items you can stock ahead:

FREEZER LIFE FOR LESS COMMON FOODS

FOOD ITEM	FREEZER LIFE MONTHS
MILK	1
KALE	2 (blanched)
BANANAS	2
CHEESE	3-4
NUTS	6-8
BUTTER	6

Here are items you should not freeze:

ITEMS YOU SHOULD NOT FREEZE

CREAM CHEESE	SOUR CREAM
RICOTTA CHEESE	COTTAGE CHEESE
COOKED EGGS	MAYONNAISE
CREAM PIES or CUSTARDS	LETTUCE

Step 2: Organize

Now that you have cleaned your freezer, it is time to get organized and optimize that space for stocking up on the best deals. You will now learn how to store all the food you brought home so that you actually want to eat it when it comes out of the freezer. The biggest objection I get about using the freezer is that the food tastes terrible once you pull it out. Keep reading, because I'll show you how to keep your food tasting great and never pay full price. The key to this is organization and proper storage—specifically, freezing your food properly and using the right types of storage containers.

Freezer Bags

I use freezer bags most frequently, because they allow me to fit more in a small amount of space. In fact, this is one of the first items that I suggest newbies stock up on. You can get a really great deal on them by combining store sales with coupons. You'll want to buy a few different sizes, including both quart- and gallon-size. Be sure you purchase "freezer" bags and not regular "sandwich" bags. Freezer bags are thicker, giving your foods more protection from freezer burn; plus, they will last longer.

LIVING *Generously* TIP

When you make a meal, cook extra and freeze to give later to someone in need.

I always double-bag the items I put into my freezer. For meats, I use a quart-sized bag to dole out family-sized portions. For instance, if I purchase five pounds of ground beef, I store one pound of meat per quart bag. Then I take all five quart bags and put them into one, gallon-sized bag. After we have consumed all the meat, I dispose of the quart bags and can reuse the gallon bag (though you never want to reuse a bag that has had raw meat in it).

Be sure to leave one-fourth to one-half inch of headspace (the space between the food and the zipper or the top of the container). Foods expand as they freeze, and you don't want the bag to burst or leak, especially if you are storing soups or stocks. You save lots of space with freezer bags because you can stack them and shape them however you want. I use freezer bags for meats, breads, odd-shaped food, fruits, and veggies.

A great way to maximize your space is to freeze items flat in the freezer bags and then stack them like books. Once frozen flat, you can move the bags around as needed. I stack them in storage bins for easy organization.

Plastic Containers

There are a few different kinds of containers you can use, but I save some of my plastic sour cream, butter, and lunchmeat tubs to reuse for storing food. If I can find clear, brand-name food storage containers for next to nothing, such as when they are on clearance and I have a coupon, I prefer them because it is easier to see what's inside.

To cut down on costs, use disposable sour cream and yogurt containers to freeze foods.

Even if the container is clear, I still label and date everything with a permanent marker (and so should you!). When you first store something, you think you will remember what it is; once it is frozen, believe me, it will look different—sometimes unrecognizable! I take a black permanent marker and write the name and date. (Remember, you want the first item in to be the first item out.) Although the date is written in permanent ink, it usually washes off so the container can be relabeled to use with another food.

I like to use plastic containers for items that are more difficult to bag or foods that might be used for lunches or meals on the go. Again, since frozen foods expand, be sure to leave a quarter- to half-inch of headspace. Plastic containers are great for soups, sauces, marinades, stocks, casseroles—anything with lots of liquid.

In addition to using larger tubs for things like soup, I use smaller containers for freezing individual servings of pizza sauce, pesto, and other types of spreads. I prefer homemade sauces, so this saves me a lot of time. I freeze items in single-serve portions (enough for one), or I freeze enough for one family-size meal. This makes it much easier when my husband wants to grab a snack while he's watching a game; he just pulls out a single-serving sauce. It's also great when I'm going to cook a quick meal, because I don't have to make the sauce; I just grab one container for an easy homemade pizza or pasta. A note of caution concerning plastic containers: do not use them to reheat items. If you are going to reheat food, be sure to put it in a glass or microwave-safe container.

Foil Pans

Use two 8x8 pans to freeze a recipe that calls for one 9x13 pan.

There are a few different ways to keep foil (aluminum) pans on hand. Foil pans are inexpensive and can be purchased from dollar stores in packs of three or four. And, as with plastic containers, you can reuse foil pans from store-bought items, like coffee cakes or casseroles. This works best when the pan is really easy to clean! If the clean-up destroys the pan, though, recycle it or use it on the grill for vegetables or delicate meats like fish.

Foil pans are also a great convenience item when I am making a meal to take to another family. This way, neither of us has to worry about me getting the pans back. These types of pans also work well if you like to do bulk cooking. You'll save lots of space and have super-easy clean-up. Typically I use two 8x8 pans to freeze a recipe that

You can find glass dishes for pennies at garage sales or thrift stores.

calls for one 9x13 pan. All I do is split the recipe into two 8x8 pans. We eat one now and freeze one for later. We have small children who are light eaters, so it works well for us right now!

When you use foil pans, try this trick to prevent freezer burn. After allowing the food to cool to room temperature, cover the dish with a layer of wax paper. (Be sure to remove the wax paper before you reheat the meal!) Then cover it with aluminum foil and/or stick the whole thing into a large, reusable freezer bag. Alternatively, you could use two layers of aluminum foil on top.

With foil pans as with other containers, be sure to leave one-quarter to one-half inch of headspace for the food to expand.

Baking Dishes

Glass or ceramic baking dishes are not ideal for the freezer, so I only use them as a last resort—for example, if I am out of foil pans or if I don't have one large enough to hold the entire meal. I line the pan with foil, put the food in it, and freeze the dish. Once the dish is frozen, I remove the meal from it and put it into a freezer bag. If it doesn't fit in a freezer bag, I just double-wrap it with aluminum foil. Then, when I want to cook the meal, I return it to the dish in which it was originally frozen.

SAVING SAVVY TIP

For easier clean-up, line pans with aluminum foil before pouring in the food.

By the way, I caution you to never put a frozen glass dish directly into a hot oven. You will end up with a shattered dish! If you choose not to use my method, be sure to slowly thaw the meal before you place the dish into the oven.

Glass dishes can last a long time and can be found at most retail stores. You can also find glass dishes for pennies at garage sales or thrift stores.

> " We buy half a cow (usually jersey) and then we're set for a long time. The steaks are so tender and the hamburger is wonderfully lean. I also freeze my garden veggies, especially green beans, red and green peppers, squash, tomatoes, etc. I don't know what I'd do without my freezer! "
>
> —Joan

Keep a Freezer Inventory

Freezer Inventory Download

Now that you have cleaned your freezer and have some space to work with, it is time to restock and make note of what you have on hand. Keep an inventory sheet of what you have in your freezer, like the one on the next page. (See the back of this book or go to FaithfulProvisions.com for additional copies.)

The Freezer Inventory List is an easy-to-use tool that tells me at a glance what is behind the freezer door. Mine is taped to the door at eye level and lists the items located inside.

To use a Freezer Inventory List, simply write the item name, quantity, date, and location of each item in your freezer. This way, you won't stand there with the door open and wonder if the frozen peas are on the bottom shelf, top shelf, or in the door, while an arctic blast chills you to the bone. Oh, and as I tell my kiddos, "Shut the door until you know what you want," because this saves energy.

Keeping your freezer full helps your items stay frozen and saves energy too. If your freezer is not full, fill milk jugs or plastic containers with water to take up the empty space.

I believe the main component to staying organized is to remember to use the inventory list. Each time I put a new item into the freezer, I write it on the list. When I pull an item out, it gets crossed off the list. You will also want to get your family on board with keeping the freezer inventory updated. I've had personal experience with what happens when they don't!

We had planned to have some guests over for hamburgers and hot dogs. So I went to my printout of the Freezer Inventory List to see how much of these items I had on hand. The list said I had plenty and there was no need for a grocery trip. A few hours before everyone arrived, I started pulling out meat and buns. Well, *someone* had forgotten to cross off the buns they had taken out for sandwiches a few weeks prior. While

faithful provisions

Freezer Inventory

Item	Qty	Location
Meats:		
Prepared Meals:		
Breads:		

Item	Qty	Location
Fruits & Veggies:		
Desserts:		
Misc:		

save money. live generously.

not the end of the world, it caused a little stress due to a last-minute trip to the grocery store. So encourage your family to cross off what they take out of the freezer to keep your inventory list accurate.

For those of you with teenagers, let's say your kiddos pull out the last frozen pizza without crossing it off the list; then a few days later their friends come over. You know that pizza you were planning on serving them? Uh-oh . . . no snacks for their friends. Use creative and supportive ways to get help in keeping your list accurate. I promise, an up-to-date freezer inventory will help everyone.

Now let's move on to how to manage the list. When your list becomes full, print a new Freezer Inventory List, and begin again. Mine is organized into categories such as meats, fruits and veggies, breads, prepared meals, and desserts. You can also use this list as a tool to jump-start your meal planning.

When you reload your freezer, arrange items in an order that makes sense to you. Put items you use a lot in your freezer where you can access them quickly—at eye level. I have an upright freezer, and I put meats on the top shelf, not only because I use them frequently but so I don't have to bend over to find them. Vegetables, fruits, and sides have their own shelf. Sweets go at the bottom—out of sight, out of mind. I also have a shelf where I store prepared meals. These can be frozen meals I have made myself, along with store-bought frozen dinners and convenience foods like waffles or veggie burgers. I love this shelf because these "go-to meals" can save the day when I haven't made a meal plan or when my plan doesn't work out (which happens more than I'd like to admit). I can walk confidently to my freezer, knowing I have a few premade meals my family can enjoy without an expensive and unplanned trip to the store or drive-through.

Flash-Freeze Foods

Flash-freezing is one of my favorite methods for storing fresh produce, meat, and baked goods until I am ready to use them. My version of flash-freezing is freezing produce, meat, or fish immediately after harvesting, butchering, or catching it, in a manner that allows you to determine the portions you need.

I frequently use this method when I find my favorite produce on sale or we're heading to a local "pick it yourself" farm. Be warned, though. If you are going to stock up on fresh produce and plan to flash-freeze it, think ahead. Don't purchase all that fresh food only to let it sit and spoil before you are able to get to it. I highly recommend freezing as soon as you can. Vegetables and fruits begin to lose their nutrients once picked. The longer they sit, the more they lose their nutritional value. If you wait too long, you might have to toss them altogether, and that would be a total waste of money.

How to
Flash-Freeze

For example, in one particularly well-watered week, our garden produced more peppers than we could eat! So I just diced them up and put them into freezer bags to use later. Flash-freezing freezes each piece separately instead of into one big lump. Fruits will be at their lowest prices during their growing season. Stock up and freeze them to enjoy all year long, using the instructions I've laid out for you on the next page, or capturing the QR code on this page with your smartphone.

HOW TO FLASH-FREEZE

1. Dice the vegetable, fruit, or meat.

2. Place the small pieces on a cookie sheet lined with wax paper.

3. Place the sheet in the freezer for 1-2 hours. Once the items are frozen, transfer them to freezer bags. Be sure to double-bag them and get all the air out!

4. Freezing this way allows you to take measuring cups and scoop out the amount you need for individual servings without dealing with big clumps of frozen food or having to unnecessarily defrost the entire portion.

Special Attention Required

One of my favorite things to flash-freeze are fresh herbs. However, herbs require a little different technique than the other foods mentioned above.

How to Flash-Freeze
Herbs

We grow a garden in the summer and I love to cook with fresh herbs, but they can be expensive. Since I have an abundance in the summer when they are at their peak, this method allows me to take advantage of my harvest all year long. Reference the instructions on the next page, or use the QR code here to make sure you get to enjoy your herbs throughout the year.

HOW TO FLASH-FREEZE HERBS

1. Put herbs through a food processor and slowly add water until they no longer stick to the sides.
2. Spoon them into an ice cube tray and freeze fully.
3. Once frozen, dump them into a freezer bag.
4. Pop them out whenever you have a recipe that calls for fresh herbs like parsley or cilantro.

What to Do If Your Freezer Goes Out

Unfortunately, even properly stored food won't stay fresh if you leave your freezer door open like I did one summer day! And I did it the day after I had hit some amazing sales on my most expensive staple items: meat and fish. I had just purchased several pounds of our favorite fish, steaks, chicken, and more. I prepared everything for the freezer, bagged it, and stored it. But early the next morning, I stepped into a puddle of water around the base of my freezer. My heart sank and I was ready to cry—actually, I did! All that time and money spent in planning and purchasing, and I was about to lose it all.

SAVING SAVVY TIP

Whenever you use dry ice, be sure to cover it in a dry towel so it does not come into direct contact with the food. This will prevent freezer burn.

Fortunately, I was blessed with a wise mother-in-law. When I called her, she advised me to run to the grocery store and purchase several packages of dry ice. By storing the food in coolers with the dry ice until the freezer was chilled again, I was able to salvage everything.

If your freezer (or electricity) actually goes out, the first thing you need to do is keep the door shut. Most freezers will keep food frozen for twenty-four to forty-eight hours if you don't let any air out and your freezer is full. Next, listen. If you don't hear the freezer running (it makes a humming sound), make sure it is plugged in and check the circuit breaker. If the breaker has been flipped, then simply turn it back on. If the freezer is still not working, you will need to move your food to coolers with dry ice and fix or replace the appliance.

Step 3: Invest in a Stand-Alone Freezer

Now that you have cleaned and organized your freezer, you will be able to take advantage of the savings you earned by storing and eating delicious meals at home. As your expertise grows, so might your need for more space. So when you are ready, it's time to think about investing in a stand-alone freezer.

Every time you close the freezer door, give it an extra push to make sure it is sealed completely.

First, though, make use of your current freezer space. Find out if you are really going to stick with this new way of shopping. The last thing I would want you to do is waste hundreds of dollars on a freezer that you may not use!

Once you have made the decision to stock ahead and purchase a freezer, you need to answer a few questions:

How Much Freezer Can You Afford?

Each household has different budgetary needs, so determine the amount you will spend. If you can't afford it, save up until you can. New freezers cost more but have warranties. Used freezers can be a good deal, but buyer beware—there is risk involved in buying a used appliance. Make sure it is clean and works properly.

How Much Freezer Space Do You Need?

How much additional freezer space do you need? A big freezer or a small one? Here is a quick guide to help you with your decision:

- ◇ compact—5 cubic feet
- ◇ small—6-9 cubic feet
- ◇ medium—12-18 cubic feet
- ◇ large—18-25 cubic feet

Where Will You Put Your Freezer?

Available space may determine the type you get. For convenience and energy savings, the best location is inside your home. We didn't have extra indoor space, so ours is in the garage.

Upright or Chest Freezer?

We chose upright because I have a bad back and this type of freezer prevents me from having to bend over to get things out. Plus, the shelves make it easy to organize.

To be fair, we have purchased two stand-alone freezers. When we initially decided to buy a freezer, we went through Craigslist and found one in our price range. We swapped some old CDs we were going to sell at a garage sale in exchange for delivery, and the unit worked great—for about nine months. Then it died. A note of caution: you can't beat the price on Craigslist, but you'll be stuck if the unit doesn't work. We replaced it with a new unit from a retail store three years ago, and it is still working well.

Generally a chest freezer can store more food, but it takes up more floor space and you can't see everything. Also, you have to bend over to get items out. You can still store a lot in upright freezers, and they take up less floor space. Also, they make organizing and clean-up easy.

WHEN CONSIDERING A FREEZER

CHEST FREEZER		UPRIGHT FREEZER	
ADVANTAGES	DISADVANTAGES	ADVANTAGES	DISADVANTAGES
ENERGY EFFICIENT	MESSY CLEAN-UP	ORGANIZATION	MORE EXPENSIVE
LESS EXPENSIVE	ORGANIZATION	USES LESS FLOOR SPACE	USES MORE ENERGY
LARGE CAPACITY	SPACE EATER	EASY TO CLEAN	
QUIET— NO FAN			

Both chest freezers and upright freezers can be purchased with a warranty at box stores or warehouse clubs. When you buy a freezer at a retail store, it's wise to ask about delivery before you purchase. Sometimes it is free within a certain area and sometimes there is a fee.

Besides filling up the fridge with on-sale meat and frozen veggies for every-day meals, I have two other main freezer savings. I wait for single-serving frozen meals to go on sale for $1.00 each and then fill up my freezer with them for my husband to take every day for lunch. I also wait for frozen pizzas to go on sale for really cheap and fill up my freezer with those. That way, we aren't tempted to order delivery when we're craving pizza!

—Ann

You have successfully made it through stocking up and freezing your foods. Now all you need to do is sort through the tools in this chapter and pick the ones that work for your lifestyle. Again, your decisions are going to rely heavily on how much time you have to invest. It's okay if you don't implement all these ideas. They are what they are . . . ideas. Take the ones that work for you and ditch the rest.

A Few Words about the Refrigerator

The refrigerator is an entirely different story. As much as I would like to only clean it when I do the freezer, I can't! It gets pretty nasty after only a few weeks.

Here are some simple strategies for cleaning your refrigerator, shelf by shelf:

1. Pull everything out of one area, shelf, or door at a time.
2. Throw away expired items.
3. Clean the shelves and all food containers with a warm, sudsy rag or vinegar cleaning solution (see recipe on page 33).
4. Restock remaining items.
5. Start over with another shelf or area.

A great way to remove food stains caused by berries, fruits, and other colored foods or drinks from the refrigerator's interior is to mix baking soda with a little water. This forms a gentle abrasive that's safe for refrigerator surfaces.

Because they have been in a constantly cold environment, you should never wash your glass or plastic refrigerator shelves in hot water. The sudden temperature change may break or crack the shelves, and then you have a whole new issue to deal with.

To stay motivated, it is best to clean shelf by shelf, or even in fifteen-minute increments. Successfully finishing one shelf at a time builds momentum and a little confidence that you can get it done! Before you know it, you have crossed off "Clean the refrigerator" from your to-do list. This method even allows you to split the project over a few days if you don't have time to clean the whole fridge at once, or if you get interrupted and need to tend to something or someone immediately.

This method is especially helpful to me because, as a mom of little kids, I never know when I am going to be called away at a moment's notice. If I am just working shelf by shelf, I can easily put things back in and see to whatever needs to be dealt with, and it isn't a big deal. On the other hand, if I pull everything out, I can't just run and do what I need to do when interrupted. This process is about doing what works for you in your season of life.

Remember, the strategies I have laid out for you in this chapter are not about doing everything at once, but about finding a system that works for you so you can begin to make a lifestyle change. It is a lasting change to your budget, not a one-off that only works sometimes. I want you to be able to save money but also keep your sanity. So the pressure is off. Implement only what you have time to do and what will help you in your home.

SAVINGS STRATEGIES FOR
YOUR FREEZER

IF YOU HAVE **MORE** TIME . . .

1. **Learn to flash-freeze foods.** This will help with ease of use and portion control.

2. **Clean and organize your freezer.** You can maximize your savings if you have room to freeze and store all the great deals you will be getting.

3. **Invest in a stand-alone freezer.** With a stand-alone freezer, you can really stock ahead with items you have saved a lot of money on.

. . . .

IF YOU HAVE *LESS* TIME . . .

1. **Use proper storage techniques.** Use the right containers to store your food in the freezer.

2. **Purge your freezer.** Discard what you don't need and make room for the great deals you will find.

3. **Create a Freezer Inventory List.** Download the Freezer Inventory List from FaithfulProvisions.com, photocopy it from the back of this book, or create your own to keep track of what's in your freezer.

Chapter 4
. . . .

PLANNING NEVER TASTED SO GOOD

It's 7:00 p.m. on a Tuesday evening and you have had a long day. The phone wouldn't stop ringing, you've been running errands all afternoon, and your meeting at church ran late, so you had to rush to pick up your daughter from school and take her to soccer practice. Or let's say you work outside the home. Your boss just asked you to add another project to your already-full plate, and you fought traffic to make it home in time for your daughter's soccer practice. Your husband arrives home after an equally challenging day. Exhausted, everyone is asking the same thing: "What's for dinner? I'm hungry."

With this question there are three possible answers:

1. "Let's go out to eat."
2. "I don't know."
3. "Let me check the meal plan. Tonight is BLTs . . . should be ready in about fifteen minutes."

Does that sound familiar? Maybe this is every night at your home (I hope not), or perhaps it occasionally happens. Either way, you would reduce your stress level and grocery budget by having a simple meal plan.

We plan our work schedules, vacations, and retirement. We plan our date nights and make schedules around TV shows and kids' activities, but we don't give a lot of time to meal planning. If you haven't thought about trying this, it can be a lifesaver for you. Why? Because meal planning is a valuable tool you can use to keep your sanity, stay organized, and save money.

What I and so many others have found is that it is critical to create a meal plan before you head to the grocery store. It can be as simple as knowing what meals you will be making, instead of just shopping for whatever your mood is. Meal planning not only resolves what you are going to fix for dinner each night, but it also helps you know what to put on your shopping list. That way, going to the grocery store isn't such a dartboard game.

By having a meal plan, I have peace of mind, feel better about what we will be eating during the week, and save so much time. Meal planning keeps me from just wandering the aisles of the grocery store and backtracking the whole time I am there.

> " *I've found meal planning to help my life all around. It helps with nutrition, variety, time, finances, and peace of mind.* "
>
> —Heather

What Is Meal Planning?

Meal planning is simply writing down the meals you intend to serve your family over a period of time. In my house, I plan meals for a week at a time. The four main components of meal planning include knowing:

- ◇ what you have on hand
- ◇ what you need
- ◇ what's on sale
- ◇ what meals you want to make

So let's get you "in the know"!

> " *I used to spend $150 a week at the grocery store for just my husband and me. I would wander around the store, usually hungry, and pick out whatever looked good. I bought way too much stuff and didn't even use it,*

resulting in a lot of waste. Meal planning helped me big time! Before I go grocery shopping, I plan a menu for the week, and I make my list from there. Having just this bit of organization really makes a difference. "

—*Brandy*

Honestly, planning ahead for my family's meals was not something I was excited about. At first it felt like another household chore, and I didn't see the value in getting organized to that degree. In my mind it was going to take a ton of work and be very time-consuming.

What I found, however, was quite the opposite. It wasn't that hard to stay organized. Also, the savings far outweighed the work I put into it. Your meal plan, and how you get there, will be unique to you and your family. What I want to do is encourage you as you get started. Take a look at the three key benefits I believe meal planning offers:

Eliminates Overbuying

Before I started meal planning, I would just pick up fresh fruits and veggies that I thought my family would enjoy that week, not taking into account how much we could *actually* eat. I quickly discovered my eyes were bigger than our stomachs!

Eliminates Waste

If you've ever thrown away food because it spoiled before it could be eaten or because you simply forgot you had it, then you have not only wasted food, you have wasted your money. As good managers of our family's resources, we do not want to be guilty of either. Meal planning enables you to make food-purchasing choices with realistic expectations about what your family will consume.

Eliminates Stress

What if you knew at breakfast what your family was going to be eating for dinner?

What if you weren't scrambling through your pantry at dinnertime, looking for something you could make quickly? What if you didn't have to order pizza three nights a week? Meal planning puts you back where you need to be: in control.

. . . .

Commit to the Lord whatever you do, and
he will establish your plans.

PROVERBS 16:3

. . . .

Plan around Your Schedule

If the thought of planning seven meals a week seems overwhelming, check your calendar. I have found that if I do this every week as I sit down to plan my trip to the grocery store, I usually don't need a full seven dinners because of other obligations and activities. If the upcoming week has scheduled activities such as travel, or the kids are at their grandparents, or we are hosting some friends for dinner, the amount of meals we need may change. Before I begin to plan my meals, I note on my meal-plan template which days I need what, and then I slot in the meals accordingly. (See the next page for a sample. You can download a free Meal-Planning Template on FaithfulProvisions.com or photocopy the one in the back of this book.)

A typical week might look like this:

faithful provisions

Meal Plan Calendar

	Week Of	
	month	day

	Dinner					Breakfast
Sunday	☑ DINE IN	☐ DINE OUT	☐ TAKEOUT			**Breakfast**
	Community Group Dinner: 15 people					banana peanut butter smoothies, toast, apples
	homemade spaghetti, green salad and bread					oatmeal, toast, strawberries
Monday	☐ DINE IN	☑ DINE OUT	☐ TAKEOUT			scrambled eggs with avocado and salsa
	Out of Town					pumpkin chocolate chip muffins, strawberry smoothies
						cereal and cantaloupe
Tuesday	☐ DINE IN	☑ DINE OUT	☐ TAKEOUT			french toast, bananas and orange juice
	Out of Town					**Lunches** tuna melts
						beef quesadillas (leftovers)
Wednesday	☐ DINE IN	☑ DINE OUT	☐ TAKEOUT			veggie burgers (freezer)
	Out of Town					spaghetti with sauce (leftovers)
						green salad with avocado and mango
Thursday	☑ DINE IN	☐ DINE OUT	☐ TAKEOUT			peanut butter sandwiches
	slow cooker carne asada					turkey sandwiches
	corn tortillas, guacamole, pico de gallo					**Snacks**
Friday	☑ DINE IN	☐ DINE OUT	☐ TAKEOUT			soft pretzels (freezer)
	homemade make-your-own pizzas					homemade popcorn
	watermelon and side salad					Shrek smoothies
Saturday	☐ DINE IN	☑ DINE OUT	☐ TAKEOUT			apples and peanut butter
	Use Groupon for Dinner					carrots and hummus

save money. live generously.

In this scenario, we are out of town three nights visiting with family, but we are scheduled to host a church group for dinner another night. I am pretty much exempt from cooking dinner most of this week, but I need to be sure to prepare for that large group on Sunday night. I don't want to have to make a pricey, eleventh-hour grocery trip, and I don't want to be stressed trying to pull together a healthy, inexpensive meal for ten people at the last minute. Sanity restored!

Meal-Planning Services

I truly hope that you'll try your hand at meal planning, but I realize that it's not for everybody. So, what do you do if you don't have time for meal planning, but you know it will save you at least 50 percent off your expenses each week? You find a good meal-planning service that plans meals and creates grocery lists for you!

Sign up for
E-Mealz.com

There are quite a few online services these days, like E-Mealz.com, that offer a variety of menu types and even stores to choose from to plan your meals and get your groceries. Most of them are a pretty good value. You typically choose your store, and the meal-planning service gives you a meal plan and grocery list according to your family size.

You don't have to be great at meal planning, but I promise you that if you incorporate meal plans into your life, you will be hooked. Anything to avoid the five o'clock stare.

Where to Start

I start my meal planning with the most expensive ingredients. These are typically my proteins. So when I sit down to create a meal plan, I plan according to what meats I already have on hand. Then I fill in with sides from there. For instance, if I go to my

Freezer Inventory Sheet and see that I have ten pounds of chicken and one pound of ground beef in my freezer, I will plan to make the majority of my meals for the week from chicken. Then I fill in my starches and vegetables with remaining stockpile items, or I will check out the grocery store sale ads to see what the best deals are.

Plan your meals from the most expensive ingredients to the least expensive ones, like this:

1. meat or proteins
2. vegetables and fresh produce
3. starches

Ingredients-Based
Recipe Index

Ingredient-Based Cooking

When it comes to meal planning, the crux of how I cook is what I call ingredient-based cooking. I stock up on ingredients I find at a great price, and then I cook and plan according to the ingredients I have on hand or what is currently on sale. To make this quite easy, you can use the Ingredient-Based Recipe Index on FaithfulProvisions .com. All you do is look up a particular ingredient, and below it you will see a list of my favorite recipes that use that ingredient.

Many grocery brands also have searchable recipe indexes on their websites. For example, Kraftrecipes.com, Kelloggs.com, and Dinner Tool.com (Proctor & Gamble) are among the manufacturer websites with online recipes that you can search by ingredient. Just look at what you have in your pantry, enter the item name on the website's recipe index, and you'll have dozens of recipes to choose from!

Even if you don't have a stock of ingredients on hand, you can still use the ingredient-based method by scanning the grocery store sales flyers and planning your meals according to what is currently on sale. Plan all your meals around the best-priced ingredients.

When meal planning, start your dinner ideas with proteins or meats you already have on hand to keep recipe costs down.

My Favorite Meal-Planning Resources

My favorite place to go for meal-planning inspiration (other than my freezer!) is online. In addition to the manufacturer websites already mentioned, there are many free online recipe sites that can help you easily and quickly plan dinner. Once you know what ingredient you want to start with, then you use the online resources to help you find easy recipes to create. Some of my favorites include:

- ◇ FoodNetwork.com
- ◇ Epicurious.com
- ◇ AllRecipes.com
- ◇ SuperCooks.com
- ◇ RecipeZaar.com

If you are looking for a more personal touch, there are some great blogs that do weekly and monthly meal planning, such as 5DollarDinners.com, OrgJunkie.com, and OnceaMonthMom.com, just to name a few.

In addition to the online resources, I love my old-fashioned cookbooks. If you don't have a copy of *Better Homes and Gardens*, it is a good, classic cookbook.[1] I enjoy putting my own twist on classics like pot roast or chicken pot pie. So I use my cookbooks to get the basic recipes and then I change them to fit my mood.

Some of my other favorite cookbooks include:

- ◇ *The Pioneer Woman Cooks*[2]
- ◇ Giada de Laurentiis (any of her books)[3]
- ◇ *Make It Fast, Cook It Slow*[4]
- ◇ Hungry Girl cookbooks[5]
- ◇ The Barefoot Contessa cookbooks[6]

Suggested Kitchen Tools and Appliances

If you seldom create your own meals, you might have to start accumulating some kitchen tools and appliances to make your kitchen time easier and more fruitful. The following are my favorites, listed in order from the most basic to ones for the more advanced cook. Many of these items you can get used at garage sales, thrift stores, and even on Craigslist.

Basics

- Cutting boards
- Sharp kitchen knives
- Baking sheets
- Mixing bowls
- Measuring cups and spoons
- Spatulas and large mixing spoons
- Baking pans—9x13, 8x8 etc.
- Pots and skillets
- Vegetable peeler, grater
- Kitchen timer (you may have one on your microwave or oven)
- Kitchen shears
- Can opener
- Slow cooker

Advanced

- Toaster oven
- KitchenAid mixer
- Bread machine
- Hand mixer
- Food processor or blender

- ◇ Cooling racks
- ◇ Electric griddle
- ◇ Wheat grinder (if you want to make homemade breads with fresh grain)
- ◇ Immersion blender
- ◇ Waffle iron

Go-To Meals

As I have mentioned, I keep a printed list of "go-to meals" on my freezer at all times. Many of you might have a similar list of your family's favorite meals in your head. This is fine, until things get busy and then you forget about what you have on hand. Your go-to meals list will tell you what is ready to serve without having to think too much.

What are go-to meals? These are the meals you typically have on hand at any time. These are the meals your family likes and eats with no complaints! In my own journey of learning how to stock up and plan ahead, I have noticed that my list of go-to meals changes according to the deals I am able to get. In this way, it evolved into a separate list from my meal plan.

Frequently, a go-to meal is incorporated into my meal plan as a backup, or for a night when we just don't feel like eating what is on the plan. A few of our go-to meals are things like tacos, pasta, or pizza. I usually have the ingredients for these meals on hand in some form. I try to balance them with healthy options. Easier said than done, but I seek to find ways to raise their nutritional content.

POPULAR GO-TO MEALS

TACOS	SPAGHETTI
PIZZA	PASTA
HAMBURGERS	MEATLOAF
ENCHILADAS	FAJITAS

For example, if my kids really want pizza (and deep down, I do too), I generally have all the ingredients for the dough and sauce. I stock up on cheese, and the other toppings depend on what I have on hand, such as sausage or ham. Then I'll add fruit, vegetables, or a green salad as a side. Now I know pizza is not the healthiest option, but in this case, I control the portions and the ingredients, and we spend less money than if we'd ordered out.

You might think making pizza dough is a deal breaker for you, but if you can spare a little time, the dough can be made easily in a bread machine or by hand. Check out my "Easy Homemade Pizza Dough" recipe in the Meal-Plan Recipe section at the back of this book. Other easy options are grabbing prepackaged dough from your grocery's refrigerated section (with a coupon), or heading to your store's bakery department to purchase handmade pizza dough. Or, if you are planning your meals and have a kitchen prep day, you can opt to make dough in advance and freeze it. We do this all the time and it works wonderfully. Whatever option you pick, you can make this a fun family night. Remember, no guilt! If your children are old enough, they can join in the prep work, and it becomes a true family meal.

HOW AND WHY TO PROOF YEAST

Why do you proof yeast?

The reason you proof yeast is to make sure it is active before you make a recipe. This way you know it will raise the dough. Yeast is a living organism, so you need to keep it in the freezer to keep it fresh. Always let it come to room temperature and never microwave it. This will kill it.

How to Proof Yeast

How to Proof Yeast

All you do to proof yeast is take your warm water and sugar quantities (already in your recipe) and mix these with the yeast in the packets (active yeast). After a few minutes, things should look creamy and foamy. Then proceed with instructions to combine ingredients.

Leave Room for Leftovers

One of the things I incorporate each week into my meal planning is a regular leftover night—we call it Smorgasbord Night. If there are several small portions of leftovers in the fridge, I will put everything out and we'll each eat a little of everything.

This serves two purposes. We are preventing waste and cleaning out the refrigerator by using what is already there. Plus, I get a night off from cooking every week, no matter what!

We also do a few other things with leftovers. Sometimes there are enough dinner leftovers for the kids and me to eat the next day for lunch. I love to take last night's leftover chicken and incorporate it into a quesadilla or salad. If you are single or like to use your freezer, you can take your leftovers and freeze single-serving portions to be eaten later for lunches, or they can be shared with a neighbor or an elderly person.

Using the Slow Cooker

My meal plan always includes at least one meal in the slow cooker (and sometimes two!) for busy days. I have a short list of tried-and-true slow cooker meals that I pull from weekly, which are based on my on-hand and on-sale lists. These are really easy meals with ingredients that can be loaded into a slow cooker to cook all day or placed into a stockpot to heat up.

I don't typically recommend using an expensive cut of meat, such as pork tenderloin or boneless chicken breast, in a slow cooker. There are many other less expensive options that usually work as well—and sometimes even better than their more expensive counterparts!

These are the cuts of meat that are well-suited to a slow cooker:

1. *Chicken*—whole chicken fryers, split chicken breasts, thighs, and drumsticks
2. *Pork*—whole pork loin and pork shoulder
3. *Beef*—chuck and top sirloin roasts

Many recipes can be easily converted to slow cooker cooking, especially soups and stews. Rice and pasta should be added the last hour of cooking, but do not decrease liquid. I've included some additional slow cooker tips on the next page.

SLOW COOKER TIPS

Trim off any visible fat from cuts of meat.
Fat will make the dishes cook faster.

Liquids do not evaporate during slow cooker cooking.

Use whole-leaf herbs and spices instead of ground herbs and spices
for better flavor. Some spices, especially pepper, can become bitter
over a long cooking time. For the best flavor, add those in the last
hour of cooking.

This chart converts oven and stove-top cooking times to slow cooker cooking times.

SLOW COOKER CONVERSION CHART

OVEN OR STOVE-TOP COOKING TIME	LOW COOKING TIME	HIGH COOKING TIME
15 to 30 minutes	4 to 8 hours	1½ to 2½ hours
35 to 45 minutes	6 to 8 hours	3 to 4 hours
50 minutes to 3 hours	8 to 16 hours	4 to 6 hours

Most uncooked meat and vegetables require a minimum of 8 hours on low.

My Big Black Book of Favorite Recipes

I have a big black three-ring binder in which I keep my most frequently used and treasured recipes, such as my favorite pizza dough, salad dressings, and casseroles. I get frustrated when I make a recipe and just love it, but then I can't find it the next time I want to make it! If a recipe is a favorite, it goes inside a plastic sheet protector. It stays in the pockets until I decide if it is worth making more than once. With my life revolving around the computer much of the time, I frequently use online recipe boxes like Ziplist.com to organize my online recipes. But if one becomes a favorite, I print it out. After all, you never know when online recipes will become unavailable for one reason or another. Plus, you might want to print out a hard copy to use while you are making the food. Even if you have a smartphone, you don't want to drip sauce all over the phone while you are reading the recipe!

My recipe binder is a great resource when I do my meal planning. Another great idea is to use a sticky note to list your most expensive ingredient items on the recipe pages. That way, when you go looking for a recipe, you can quickly see if it would be a meal you can incorporate into that week's plan.

To aid in meal planning, use sticky notes on recipe pages to list the most expensive ingredients.

Here's a scenario: if I am making chicken enchiladas, I might put things like cooked chicken, enchilada sauce, and flour tortillas on the note. Those items are necessary to make that dish, and they can drive up the cost of the meal. If I don't already have the items on hand, I might hold off and incorporate that meal later, once I have purchased the ingredients during a great sale.

Another thing I have learned is to wait to make a new recipe until I am able to purchase the ingredients when they are on sale. I am forever finding great new recipes to try. I used to watch the Food Network, see a demonstration, and head straight to the grocery to purchase everything in the meal. Then I realized that I was spending close to thirty dollars per meal for two adults! Now when I see a new recipe, whether it is on a cooking show or published online, I hang on to it and, as with my favorite recipes, determine the most expensive ingredients. I put the ingredients that I don't have on my stockpile list so I can keep an eye out for them to go on sale. Using this method, I plan my new recipes in advance, only making them when I have been able to get the ingredients at the best possible price. Sometimes this means as much as a 75 percent savings on the meal! Planning ahead and using self-control can save you a lot of money, time, and stress.

Transitioning into a Lifestyle of Meal Planning

While I was teaching a workshop last week, a woman asked me a question that might be helpful to answer for you. She said she and her family eat out three meals a day. The concept of cooking, let alone meal planning, was completely foreign to her. Since she doesn't usually cook, stockpile, or plan meals, there was no way she could just hit the ground running with all the savvy saving concepts. So what should she do?

My recommendation to her was to pick two easy meals a week and plan them from ingredients that are on sale in a local grocery store's sale ad. This way she doesn't have to stock ahead or even use coupons if she isn't ready.

By beginning with the basics, starting small and doing what you can, you build a sense of confidence in meal planning. That is very important when beginning something new. Start by making small changes so you can see the benefits. Then you'll have the confidence and experience to take all the tools of saving to new heights!

Managing Your Meal Plan

Again, with the idea being not to pay full price, I plan my meals around two things: the items I already have on hand and the steals I can find each week at the grocery. My goal is to write my meal plan *while* I am doing my grocery planning.

To get you started, let me show you a couple of weekly meal plans from my kitchen. Beginning with a snapshot of my weekly grocery trip, here are a few deals I was able to snag:

- Three, three-pound bags of organic potatoes (using a rain check)
- Four packages of bacon (using coupons combined with a store sale)
- Three packages of chicken for less than $1.00/pound (sales combined with coupons)
- Two packages of pork chops (marked down as "manager's specials")

Here is how I incorporated the above items with what I already had on hand.

Sample Meal Plan Week #1

Sunday: Baked ziti with green salad, garlic bread, and brownies

I prepared a meal for a large group from our church. To feed this crowd, I wanted to use what I already had on hand, plus I wanted to go meatless to keep the cost down. Of course, I wanted to serve something that everyone would like that was also tasty and filling! I had pasta, pasta sauce, and brownie mix in my pantry. The only thing I had to purchase to make the main dish was the ricotta cheese. I had bought garlic bread for twenty-five cents at Publix the week before, and I had a huge bag of lettuce, as well as some organic carrots and tomatoes from my garden (my pantry stays full of salad dressing), so then I just made iced tea (from my almost-free tea bags), and we were ready to eat. That meal only cost me about two dollars for ten people, and the crowd loved it!

Monday: Chicken pot pie soup with green salad and biscuits sprinkled with chili powder

Combining a coupon with a store sale, I was able to get brand-name chicken the week before for less than a dollar per pound. I still had the bagged lettuce for the salad. The canned biscuits came from a store savings event, which again combined with coupons for a great deal! I cooked a little extra chicken to use for our BBQ chicken pizza scheduled for Friday.

Tuesday: BLT sandwiches with carrot salad and ginger dressing

The week I did this meal plan, there were some printable manufacturer's coupons

that, combined with a local store sale, made a package of bacon free. I cooked extra at breakfast and used the leftovers in BLTs. At the time, I also had lots of tomatoes ripe from the garden and still plenty of lettuce.

To save money on meat, purchase it whole and then ask the butcher to cut it into steaks. Most grocery stores offer this service to their customers for free.

Wednesday: Grilled tilapia with rice and steamed broccoli

I had purchased frozen fish when it was at its rock-bottom price of $2.99/pound, so I had it on hand in my freezer. I used my almost-free rice packets and frozen broccoli I had snagged for twenty-five cents to make this meal. I also cooked extra so we could have an easy meal for tomorrow: fish tacos. I even grilled the corn ahead too, since the grill was already fired up.

Thursday: Fish tacos with grilled corn and watermelon

I used the fish and corn that I grilled Wednesday night, then I sliced the watermelon that was on sale. The hardest thing about this dinner was assembling the tacos, wrapping them in foil with the corn, and popping them in the toaster oven to heat through—pretty easy.

Friday: Grilled rib eye steak with baked potatoes, green salad, and bread

I had purchased our favorite—rib eye—the week before this meal plan for about $4.88/pound. It is much cheaper when you purchase it whole and have the butcher cut it into steaks. Most grocery stores offer this service free as a courtesy to their customers.

Saturday: Homemade barbecue chicken pizza with green salad and fries

Pizza is a family favorite and a staple for us most weekends. I make homemade pizza dough ahead of time and freeze it, then the toppings depend on what we have still available from the week. In this case, I had cooked extra chicken earlier in the week to use for this barbecue chicken pizza. I usually include some kind of vegetable side and even fruit if it works well with the meal.

Sample Meal Plan Week #2

Sunday: Sirloin pork chops with baked potatoes, sliced tomatoes, and sautéed garden squash

My local store had the pork chops marked down as a "manager's special," so I got two packages and cooked them both. This meal plan shows one package being used for Sunday dinner. Later in the week, I scheduled a meal of pork fried rice. A portion of the pork was used to make quesadillas for lunch. I still had organic potatoes, lots of tomatoes, and a little squash from the garden.

Monday: Chili pot roast with mashed potatoes, peas, and green salad

I cooked a five-pound pot roast in my slow cooker, then portioned out the meat to use for this meal and two others: beef empanadas and French dip sandwiches.

Tuesday: Pork fried rice with carrot salad with ginger dressing and egg rolls

I cubed the pork from Sunday's meal and used the shredded organic carrots I got last week on sale in the fried rice and to make a side salad. Sometime before this week's meal plan, I had gotten a great deal on some egg rolls (stored in my freezer), and they rounded out this meal nicely.

Double recipes and freeze the extras in disposable containers to give to a new mom or to someone who is going through a difficult time.

Wednesday: French dip sandwiches with steak fries and watermelon

The chili pot roast left me with lots of leftover pulled beef, so I incorporated some of the meat into my French dip sandwiches. (My husband loves these!) I finished off one bag of organic potatoes for this meal, cutting them into steak fries, and that still left me with a bag of premade steak fries to put in the freezer for later use. Again, I chose watermelon as my fruit. Because it was in season at the time, I purchased it at a rock-bottom price. It's a family favorite, and we had a large one to get through!

Thursday: Smorgasbord Night

Because I was teaching a workshop across town on this particular night, I'd planned for plenty of leftovers from the previous nights' meals. Dinner was a breeze with easy clean-up, resulting in less stress as I headed out the door!

Friday: Pizza Margherita with watermelon and grapes

Pizza night! I pulled out my frozen pizza dough that afternoon to thaw on the counter. Since we had plenty of tomatoes and fresh basil in the garden I chose to make a Pizza Margherita, and then added the fruit I had on hand for sides.

Saturday: Beef empanadas with green salad, tomatoes, and balsamic dressing

We love beef empanadas, and I usually make them with pie crust. However, instead of buying pie crust at full price, I improvised this week and used the crescent rolls I had purchased (on sale and with a coupon) for twenty-five cents each. Again, eating from the surplus we had on hand, I made a green salad with tomatoes, this time adding a homemade balsamic dressing. (This dressing works well with the light taste in the empanadas.)

Sample Breakfast, Lunch, and Snack Meal Plan

In addition to planning our dinners, I lay out what types of meals I can pull together for breakfast, lunch, and snacks. More than anything, this is just a list of ideas so I don't have to think too hard! I look at the list, already knowing that I have these items on hand, and I go from there, marking off the items as they are eaten. (See next two pages.)

Have a Kitchen Prep Day

One of my favorite ways to make my meal planning easier is to plan a kitchen prep day. Now I know a lot of you are reading and thinking, *Are you crazy?*, or *I am glad she has that kind of time.* I am not talking about setting aside an entire day (unless you want to). For me, a kitchen prep day just means setting aside an hour or two to prepare or put away foods that our family frequently eats or that are perishable. It can include flash-freezing bananas for smoothies or making a big batch of home-made pizza dough to freeze for later. If you are really ambitious, you can even turn it into a "once-a-month cooking day" to cook all your meats, dole them into various entrees, and then freeze them for your family to eat during the month. Whatever you decide, the most important part is that you have a plan for what you are going to do.

Kitchen Prep Day
List

faithful provisions

Meal Plan Calendar

Week Of

month   day

Dinner				Breakfast
Sunday	☑ DINE IN	☐ DINE OUT	☐ TAKEOUT	**Breakfast**
Community Group Dinner: 10 people				banana peanut butter smoothies, toast, apples
baked ziti, green salad, garlic bread, brownies				oatmeal, toast, strawberries
Monday	☑ DINE IN	☐ DINE OUT	☐ TAKEOUT	scrambled eggs with avocado and salsa
chicken pot pie soup				pumpkin chocolate chip muffins, strawberry smoothies
green salad, biscuits				cereal, cantaloupe
Tuesday	☑ DINE IN	☐ DINE OUT	☐ TAKEOUT	French toast, bananas and orange juice
BLT sandwiches				**Lunches** tuna melts
carrot salad with ginger dressing				beef quesadillas (leftovers)
Wednesday	☑ DINE IN	☐ DINE OUT	☐ TAKEOUT	veggie burgers (freezer)
grilled tilapia with rice				spaghetti with sauce (leftovers)
steamed broccoli with lemon butter sauce				green salad with avocado and mango
Thursday	☑ DINE IN	☐ DINE OUT	☐ TAKEOUT	peanut butter sandwiches
fish tacos: corn tortillas, fish, cabbage, crema, lime				turkey sandwiches
chile lime corn and watermelon				**Snacks**
Friday	☑ DINE IN	☐ DINE OUT	☐ TAKEOUT	soft pretzels (freezer)
grilled rib eye steak with loaded baked potato				homemade popcorn
green salad, homemade bread				Shrek smoothies
Saturday	☑ DINE IN	☐ DINE OUT	☐ TAKEOUT	apples and peanut butter
homemade BBQ chicken pizza				carrots and hummus
green salad and homemade sweet potato fries				

 save money. live generously.

faithful provisions

Meal Plan Calendar

Week Of

month | day

	Dinner				Breakfast	
Sunday	☑ DINE IN	☐ DINE OUT	☐ TAKEOUT			
	sirloin pork chops with baked potatoes				freezer waffles with strawberries	
	sliced tomatoes, sauteed garden squash				strawberry smoothies, whole wheat toast, peanut butter	
Monday	☑ DINE IN	☐ DINE OUT	☐ TAKEOUT		cereal, whole wheat toast with jelly, apples and grapes	
	chili pot roast with cream cheese mashed potatoes				pumpkin chocolate chip muffins, strawberry smoothies	
	green salad and peas				breakfast burrito (egg, cheese, salsa) and fruit	
Tuesday	☑ DINE IN	☐ DINE OUT	☐ TAKEOUT		oatmeal, bananas and orange juice	
	pork fried rice with egg rolls			**Lunches**	tuna melts	
	carrot salad with ginger dressing				tomato sandwiches, watermelon slices	
Wednesday	☑ DINE IN	☐ DINE OUT	☐ TAKEOUT		grilled cheese, tomatoes, sliced apples	
	French dip sandwiches				leftovers: pork fried rice, chili pot roast	
	steak fries and watermelon				green salad with avocado and mango	
Thursday	☑ DINE IN	☐ DINE OUT	☐ TAKEOUT		peanut butter sandwiches, sliced apples	
	Smorgasboard Night				turkey sandwiches	
	Leftovers!			**Snacks**		
Friday	☑ DINE IN	☐ DINE OUT	☐ TAKEOUT		cheese slices on crackers	
	pizza margherita				homemade popcorn	
	watermelon, grapes				Shrek smoothies	
Saturday	☑ DINE IN	☐ DINE OUT	☐ TAKEOUT		apples and peanut butter	
	beef empanadas				carrots and hummus	
	green salad with tomatoes and balsamic dressing				applesauce, yogurt, or string cheese	

save money. live generously.

First, you must know it is all about the planning. Without a plan, you can potentially waste a lot of precious time and effort. For instance, you might be in the middle of your cooking and realize you are out of an ingredient, and have to make a last-minute trip to the store. This negates the time you planned to save. If you don't have all the ingredients and tools you need, it can make things difficult. So, in order to make your kitchen prep day successful—whether big or small—here are some tips to help you out.

A few days before you plan your prep day, do the following:

- *Make a menu.* Make an exhaustive list of all the items you want to make during your prep-day time.

- *Gather the recipes.* Pull a recipe for each menu item you want to make. Read through them and get an idea of oven temps, mixing bowls, and other items that you might need across the different recipes.

- *Write a shopping list.* Read through each recipe and make a list of all the items you don't have on hand. Even if you think you have vanilla, be sure to double-check that you have enough for each recipe. Trust me, I have had to go to the grocery right in the middle of a prep day. Not fun.

- *Have a prep list.* Look through each recipe and create a step-by-step plan of each thing you need to do. For example, cut onions, shred cheese, etc.

- *Have a plan for your kids (if you have them).* You have a couple of options here. Option 1: If you have a parent, a sister, or someone who can play with the children while you are working, that is best. Option 2: Plan ways to incorporate the kids in your day by helping, or have activities they can do while you work.

- *Finalize the master plan.* At this point, you are just listing in order all the tasks you need to do to get each recipe completed. For instance, after you make the muffin mix and put it in the oven, start mixing the dough for cinnamon rolls.

◇ *Grocery shop.* Make your final grocery trip and get ready to cook!

Meal Planning Works

I believe meal planning is the most effective way to reduce your grocery costs. After only three months of consistent weekly meal planning, I reduced our weekly grocery budget by 50 percent! If you like what you've learned in this chapter, you will find more helpful hints at my website, FaithfulProvisions.com. You can check out my online Recipe Box for my full stock of recipes. Also, you'll find the recipes used in these two weeks' worth of meal plans in the appendix. Enjoy!

Faithful Provisions Recipe Box

SAVINGS STRATEGIES FOR
MEAL PLANNING

IF YOU HAVE **MORE** TIME . . .

1. **Use ingredient-based recipes.** Plan your meals around the ingredients you have in your pantry and freezer.

2. **Purchase kitchen appliances and tools.** Be sure to stock your kitchen with the proper items to help make your kitchen time more fruitful.

3. **Manage meal planning.** Reference the sample weekly meal plans in this chapter, and use the template in the back of this book or at FaithfulProvisions.com to get you started.

IF YOU HAVE **LESS** TIME . . .

1. **Plan around your calendar.** Be sure to meal plan around your schedule. Many times you don't need a meal every night.

2. **Use a meal-planning service.** Use a service like E-Mealz.com to make your meal planning easy!

3. **Know your "go-to" meals.** Create a list of your family's favorite meals and keep supplies on hand for those meals.

4. **Use the slow cooker.** If you don't have a slow cooker, it's worth the investment. The easiest meal planning tool is putting things in the cooker and letting it cook all day, so dinner is ready when you come home.

5. **Be creative with leftovers.** Use what is in your fridge to save money and time.

Chapter 5

I'VE GOT A COUPON
FOR THAT

Using coupons is a great way to decrease your spending and increase your savings by 75 percent or more. You've already learned the principle of stocking ahead: purchasing items at their lowest prices and purchasing in large enough quantities to get you through to the next sale. Couponing, however, is the icing on the cake of savings. You create the lowest price by combining sale ads with savvy coupon usage to reach rock-bottom prices.

Using coupons may not be for everyone. Depending on your circumstances, you just may not have the time or resources for couponing. Still others see couponing as a lot of trouble. In fact, when I teach on saving money with coupons, I often receive the following feedback: "I took my coupons when I went grocery shopping, and the store brand was still cheaper than the name brand combined with a coupon! The effort to coupon just isn't worth it. By simply purchasing store brands, I can save plenty." The key to using coupons is to be strategic about your usage. It certainly does require you to work a little bit harder, but that work comes in being organized and planning your shopping trips. Using a coupon on a full-priced item is not a good savings strategy.

You might also tell yourself, "There aren't any coupons for the things that I need." I hear this a lot from people who haven't yet experienced the benefits of couponing. Remember, couponing is saving you money. It is like using cash to get deeper savings in the checkout line. While I agree there is an abundance of coupons available for things you may not think you need or want (at first glance), here are a few questions I urge you to ask yourself:

- ◊ Will my family use this product regardless of the brand?
- ◊ If I get it free, will we use it?
- ◊ Can we donate this item to an individual or organization?

If you answered "yes" to all three of these questions, then couponing is for you. I have found, at the very least, that when it comes to coupons, the offers are usually for something I can donate, which gives me an opportunity to live generously!

Name Brand versus Store Brand

I only use coupons when I can combine them with a sale or with other rebate programs. For instance, if name-brand peanut butter is regularly $2.49, and I have a coupon for $1 off, I can almost always get the store brand for the same price or cheaper, without the effort of using coupons.

Name-Brand Peanut Butter—regular price $2.49

Use $1/1 Name-Brand Peanut Butter Coupon

Final Price: $1.49 after coupon alone

However, if the name-brand peanut butter is on sale for $1.49, and I have a coupon for $1 off, then I have gotten a rock-bottom price of 49 cents that I could never get without using a coupon on a store-brand item.

Name-Brand Peanut Butter—on sale $1.49

Use $1/1 Name-Brand Peanut Butter Coupon

Final Price: $.49 after coupon and sale

So, as you can see from the scenarios above, you are much better off purchasing the name-brand products *when they are on sale* and pairing them with a coupon to save big. If there are no sales to go with my coupons, I almost exclusively purchase store-brand products.

Using coupons is a great way to stock up on your staple items, especially if you have more than one coupon for an item. You can use one manufacturer coupon per item, so the more coupons you have, the more items you can purchase. Just make sure the coupon specifies "per item." If it is "per purchase," you may need to make multiple purchases. I suggest starting out obtaining one coupon insert per family member through your local paper. Once your stockpile has reached a nice level, then you can back off.

A Savings Scenario

Check out this savings scenario: When I have two coupons for brand-name canned tomatoes and they go on sale, I can get two cans of tomatoes at the rock-bottom price, instead of just one. I have found this to be one of the best ways to fill my pantry, fridge, and freezer at the lowest prices. Here is the math:

Buy 2 Name-Brand Tomatoes @ $.70/ea = $1.40

Use [2] $.55/1 Name-Brand Tomatoes Coupons

Final Price: $.15 each when you buy two after sale and coupon

Note: The $.55/1 means it is 55 cents off when you buy one. If it is $.55/2, that means 55 cents off when you buy two items.

The most important tip to making coupon usage easier is to be organized. Recently I was chatting with a friend who was so excited because she was going to start using coupons! She was telling me about how she had collected so many already, and I asked her what she had gotten. She proceeded to open a kitchen drawer filled with loose coupons! If that is the way you are going to use coupons, I highly recommend just tracking sales and buying loss leaders—those deeply discounted products that stores sell to get customers in the door. You will be happier and less frustrated. The point of using coupons is to save more money by being savvy about saving. You don't want to waste your precious time rifling

If there are no sales to go with my coupons, I almost exclusively purchase store-brand products.

through scads of coupons looking for that one you can't find! So the first thing I stress when it comes to using coupons is organization.

· ·

Who then is the faithful, thoughtful, and wise servant, whom
his master has put in charge of his household to give to
the others the food and supplies at the proper time?

MATTHEW 24:45 AMP

· ·

To Clip or Not to Clip?

"Coupon clipping has gotten a bum rap as a fool's pastime," says award-winning writer Denise Topolnicki, author of *How to Raise a Family on Less than Two Incomes*. While she advocates the use of coupons and takes advantage of them herself, she aptly describes how many people feel when it comes to clipping these little gems.

Couponing is a great way to save money, though as with anything, it has its pros and cons. Here are some of those, directly from my blog readers!

Pros of Clipping Coupons

Save money. This is the ultimate goal; being savvy with your coupon strategies will allow you to save tons.

Get free items. I think the biggest pro is being able to grab things for free. Even if you don't need them, you can donate them to someone who does.

Replace income. The art of couponing can be such that it becomes like a new part-time job. Yes, it is work, but for many it is well worth it. For instance, it is a great option for those who choose to stay home with their children or for individuals who have hit retirement age.

Increase giving. One of the unknown benefits of couponing is your ability to bless others and increase your giving capacity. By purchasing items at 75 percent off or getting them free, the act of giving with a joyful heart is much more frequent.

Bless others. You can bless military families overseas by sending your expired coupons for them to use on international military bases (check out OCPnet.org or Coupons ToTroops.com). So, by couponing, you understand what a blessing it can be to others.

Cons of Clipping Coupons

The coupon "high." Sometimes buyers get hooked on the "high" of saving money. It becomes an addiction and they end up using coupons on things they don't really need, just to save money. If you're buying stuff with coupons that you don't need (or don't plan to give away), then you're not saving money.

Unhealthy choices. Many coupons are for prepackaged foods, which are often considered unhealthy. If you want to eat healthy and also use coupons, you can do that with good planning. Purchasing unhealthy food with a coupon is no bargain! (This is why meal planning—explained in chapter 4—is so important!)

Long checkouts. When you use coupons, the time it takes you at checkout may bring a few new challenges.

Time-consuming. Especially in the beginning you can spend a lot of time clipping and organizing your coupons. This will get better.

Eating Healthy While Couponing

As I talk to readers online or speak with workshop attendees, a concern many have is that coupons are mostly for processed foods. So the argument is that the only way they can save big is by purchasing processed food. That was the case when I started couponing because my mind-set was first about saving money and *then* feeding my family healthy food options. However, over the years, I have shifted my focus and now feel that the most important thing is offering my family healthy options *while* saving money. I am not saying I don't occasionally buy processed food, but the majority of my purchases are healthier choices.

Another thing you need to know is that when you see shows like The Learning Channel's *Extreme Couponing* and read many extreme couponing blogs, most of the purchases being made don't include fresh produce and meats. So you have to balance it out a bit and have a reasonable expectation. You can't spend ten dollars a week and feed your family healthy meals. But you can expect to greatly decrease your spending by using coupons strategically, meal planning, and stocking up on healthy options.

LIVING *Generously* TIP

Use coupons to get free and extra items to give to those in need.

These days there are coupons available for natural, healthy, and even organic items. You can find these coupons online and in the weekly Sunday coupon inserts. On FaithfulProvisions.com, we have a whole page of manufacturers' and couponing websites where you can print and request coupons for organic and all-natural products. Pair those with store sales and markdowns, and you can stock up. Over the past several years my family has started incorporating organic options into our meals and we didn't have to increase our budget significantly. Our overall budget only went up by about 20 percent. If you are going all organic, that might change, but if you are doing a little here and there, you can fully expect to save while couponing.

Manufacturer Coupons

There are two types of coupons you may use on items at the grocery store: manufacturer coupons and store coupons. No matter where you got them, every coupon is put out by either a manufacturer or a retail store.

Manufacturer coupons are circulated by the makers of specific products. These are found in many different places, such as:

- Sunday newspapers
- magazines
- manufacturers' websites
- store coupon booklets
- coupon websites (such as Coupons.com, RedPlum.com and Smart-source.com)
- "blinkie" red machines attached to the shelf
- catalinas available at checkout on your register receipt
- sale ads

The Sunday Newspaper

The most common place for finding a large number of manufacturer coupons at one time is still the Sunday paper. If you haven't already subscribed, consider getting a Sunday subscription to your local paper. Newspapers are doing everything they can these days to gain readers, and you can find deals on a subscription for the Sunday editions only. I recommend that you subscribe to your local paper, especially when you are first starting to collect and use coupons. This will help you get used to needing the paper each week. Also, if you forget to pick up a Sunday paper, you will miss out unless you have a subscription.

As you are beginning to stock up, I highly recommend getting more than one Sunday paper. Having more coupons means more deals. There are usually two to three coupon inserts in the Sunday paper each week. One way to do this is to buy an extra paper per family member.

Now, you might be thinking that is a waste of paper. If you do, here is a solution: collect unwanted coupon inserts from friends and family. You will be amazed at the people you know who throw out the Sunday coupon inserts each week. My mother-in-law knows I clip coupons, so each time she comes over she has in hand a stack of the latest coupon inserts. She has even started helping me by grabbing a few from her friends to give to me!

Multiple Sunday Inserts

I recommend that you purchase one Sunday newspaper coupon insert per family member. In order to save the most, you want to get multiples of items when they are on sale so you can stock up. You may only use one manufacturer coupon per item, so the more coupons you have, the more of an item you can purchase while it is on sale. Some stores limit the number of "like" coupons you can use per transaction, so be sure to check before you purchase multiple inserts.

All You Subscription
Page

Magazines

I'm finding that more and more magazines are carrying manufacturer's coupons. Be on the lookout! My favorite magazine for coupons is *All You* magazine. Check out FaithfulProvisions.com for details on how and where to get these high-value magazine coupons.

Coupon Websites

Here is a list of some websites that have printable or loadable manufacturer's coupons. Due to the nature of the Internet, these sites change periodically. This list can be a starting point for you.

- ◊ Coupons.com—up to 150 printable coupons each month that can be printed twice per computer.
- ◊ SmartSource.com—pages of manufacturer coupons that reset each month; these can also be printed twice per coupon.

- RedPlum.com—printable manufacturer coupons that frequently change through the month.
- Cellfire.com—coupons can be downloaded to your store loyalty card or cell phone.
- Shortcuts.com—coupons can be downloaded to your store loyalty card. There is a limit to the amount of coupons you can load per month, so choose wisely.
- Upromise.com—e-coupons can be downloaded to a variety of store loyalty cards. These do not take amounts off at checkout. Rather, the amount you load is dropped into a college savings account.

Store Coupons

Store coupons are coupons that are offered by retail stores. These are typically not put out by the manufacturers of the products, but by the stores themselves. Coupons from the stores can be found in a variety of places. Many print store coupon booklets, distribute weekly sales flyers with coupons, and even have lots of printable coupons on the store's website.

Weekly Sale Ads

In addition to finding the store sales items in the weekly sale ads, some stores even offer store coupons within their ads. Typically if they are in the store's weekly sale ad, they will expire once the ad expires.

Store Loyalty Programs

One of my best sources for store coupons are store loyalty programs. Store loyalty programs are typically maintained by a shopper's card, which entitles the bearer to special discounts. But many other stores have loyalty programs like baby clubs, senior days, and even seafood clubs. One of our local stores even tracks my buying and sends me store coupons for the items I purchase the most. This is a great way to obtain many different forms of store coupons, both paper and printable. At your store's customer service desk, ask what types of customer loyalty programs they have available. I also highly recommend signing up for anything you can on the store's website. I get lots of coupons mailed to me this way.

SAVING SAVVY TIP

When you sign up for online loyalty programs, use a junk e-mail address (e.g., mycoupons@ yahoo.com).

The most popular type of loyalty program is with a store card or loyalty card. It's usually a key tag that fits on your key chain (my husband calls my key chain "the nunchucks" because there are so many key tags, it looks like a weapon—a weapon of savings, I remind him) and is scanned before your purchases. Some stores use this to bring you everyday store discounts, discounts on a specific product weekly, or even to give you a percentage off your total purchase, depending on when you shop at their store.

If you go to most grocery store websites, you can sign up for other types of loyalty programs, which will get your name on their mailing lists. This gets paper coupons sent to your mailbox, and also e-mailed to your inbox. I find that these tend to be the best coupons I get. Typically, these are of higher value and targeted to my personal everyday purchases. Also you can write to a manufacturer and provide specific feedback about a product, and they will sometimes mail great coupons to you.

Competitors' Coupons

Some stores will even accept competitors' store coupons. I really like this policy because it allows me to get more deals in one store, rather than running to several different stores. It makes things easier for me, which means more sales for them! If your store accepts competitors' coupons you need to go to the customer service desk to ask which stores they consider competitors and what their store policy is on taking competitors' coupons. Also, ask if they will take online printable coupons and find out if there are any restrictions. I have found that while some grocery store chains take competitors' coupons, the stores they consider competitors will vary depending on the neighborhood, city, county, or state.

Store Coupon Booklets

Another great source for coupons are the coupon booklets grocery stores publish. These usually coincide with sales, which can add up to even bigger savings. I pick up two (just as I buy two to three Sunday papers), and I keep these with my coupons so that as I prepare my weekly shopping list, I can look back through them. Grocery store coupon booklets are found at the front of the store either in their own wire racks or on the same shelving where you find the store's weekly sale ads. Many manufacturers will set up in-store displays where you can pick up an entire booklet or pull coupons off a tear pad. These booklets can be store and manufacturer coupons, depending on who published the booklet.

Please don't be a booklet hoarder! Grocery store coupon booklets go fast, and I think it is because many people take more than they truly need. I admit that early on, I was one of those people. I have learned, though, that part of living generously includes stocking up on only what I reasonably need and leaving deals for others. To do anything more than this is hoarding. Hoarding robs others of an opportunity to save money while providing for their families. It also takes away their opportunity to be blessed by giving. I try to keep in mind that God will provide all my needs—with or without those coupon booklets!

· ·

[Jesus] said to them, "Watch out! Be on your
guard against all kinds of greed; life does not
consist in an abundance of possessions."

LUKE 12:15

· ·

Loadable Coupons

With e-coupons, also called digital coupons, there's nothing to clip and organize. You simply download all your coupons to your account prior to going to the store, and when the cashier scans your loyalty card, the discounts automatically come off your purchase and show up on your receipt. Easy! Beware, though. Once you load coupons onto your account, you usually can't take them off. If the card has a maximum number of coupons you can load per month, be sure you load only the ones you know you will use and leave a few spaces open for those last-minute purchases where you will need a little extra discount!

Loadable coupons *do not* double, like printable coupons can. These coupons are usually redeemed at face value. Plus if you have a paper coupon that is a higher value than your loadable coupon, most stores' computers are set up to use the loadable coupon first. So you need to be careful about planning before you go to the store. This is an area of couponing where the rules and policies are frequently changing, so be sure to check with your local store to see what their policies are.

When you use your store card and purchase an item for which you've downloaded a coupon, the amount of the coupon will automatically come off your purchase. Currently, the main portals for loadable coupons to store cards are Cellfire.com and Shortcuts.com. Just log on to the loadable coupon website and set up a free account. Enter your store loyalty card number (the long number under the bar code) when prompted, then select the coupons you want loaded. Note that it typically takes twenty-four to forty-eight hours for the coupons to be available in the system for you to use at checkout. However, with all the smartphone technology, many loadable coupon sites now have smartphone apps where you can load the coupons to your card while you are at the store! Usually these will be available within fifteen to twenty minutes of loading.

Tips for Using Loadable e-Coupons or Digital Coupons

Many of us go online and load the e-coupons at the beginning of each month and don't really track them at checkout. With stores changing policies on loadable coupon usage, you have to be strategic when loading your coupons to your cards. I recommend only loading the ones you know you want to use, because if you get to checkout and you have a paper coupon with a higher value, the e-coupon will come off instead.

My theory is that sometimes this can be more hassle than the value of the loadable coupon is worth, since e-coupons do not double.

Here are a few tips to help you in being strategic when using loadable coupons.

1. **Don't load e-coupons at all.** While I love the additional savings that e-coupons can bring, I only use them because they are easy. If they become difficult to use I will most likely quit loading them, unless they significantly raise their value.

2. **Print a list of e-coupons from your card.** Before heading out or even planning, print out a list of all the e-coupons you load to your shopper's card. This way you know which e-coupons are actually on your card, and you can plan accordingly while you are at home.

3. **Remove unwanted e-coupons.** If you are planning your trip and determine that there are e-coupons you don't want to use, some e-coupon sites will allow you to remove them. However, there are a few that you cannot remove once loaded.

4. **Drop by customer service after checking out.** At checkout if you find your paper coupon is a higher value than your e-coupon, I recommend

heading to the customer service desk to let them know you would like to use the paper coupon instead. I can't guarantee they will oblige, but if stores find they are having issues with certain policies, this is a good way to let them know!

Coupon Printing Tips

One of the first things you will notice in your couponing journey is the plethora of online printable coupons. Printing them can be a huge expense unless you are smart about it.

Here are a few of my favorite ways to help you lower the costs associated with printing online coupons. These will help you save ink, toner, money, time, and frustration.

Use economy, fast draft, or draft quality settings. This can cut back as much as 50 percent of the ink used in each print session. You do need to be careful and make sure the quality isn't so bad that the coupons won't scan at the checkout. If that happens, you need to bump up the quality to the next setting.

Set printer defaults to "black ink only." Set your printer defaults to black ink only. Color ink is much more expensive, and stores will accept coupons whether they are printed in black ink or color. With many printers and computers you have to preset this; you can't set it to print for each selection of coupons. It needs to be your printer's default setting.

Recycle paper. I always try to recycle paper by using the flipside for printing my coupons. Stores don't care (and neither do I!) what is on the back of the coupon. They just need the coupon barcode to scan at checkout. I collect old mail and any paper I am going to discard. I am amazed at how many pieces of paper I can recycle for this purpose. Recycling paper saves me even more money!

Recycle empty ink cartridges. Find out what ink cartridge recycling programs are offered at your local office supply stores, such as OfficeMax, Office Depot, and Staples. For example, I know Staples' Rewards program currently gives you two dollars for each ink cartridge you bring in to recycle, with a maximum per month. This really helps in bringing down my out-of-pocket costs on ink. When you find them, you can also use coupons and rebate programs to stock up on ink. Then there's Cartridge World, which not only gives you a discount for recycling but sells replacement cartridges at a significant savings. All of these places give smart shoppers the opportunity to buy low and be green at the same time.

Stack Coupons for Greater Savings

Learning to stack coupons was a watershed moment in my couponing journey. I felt like the curtain had been pulled back when I learned this wonderful secret! Stacking coupons is using a manufacturer coupon *and* a store coupon together on one item. By stacking coupons, you can get great prices on items that aren't even on sale. But of course the best use of stacking is when an item is on sale, on clearance, and/or has rebates associated with it.

Stack a manufacturer coupon with a store coupon on a sale item to save the most.

Check out the deal scenario below on a box of Cheerios regularly priced at $3.99 per box on sale for just $1.99, to see how it works.

Cheerios—on sale for $1.99

Use $.55/1 Cheerios coupon 12/10/2010 SS insert (manufacturer coupon)

Use $1/1 Cheerios Store Coupon (printable or in-store booklet or flyer)

Final Price: $.44 after sale, store, and manufacturer coupon

After the sale, store, and manufacturer coupons you are able to get a regularly priced box of Cheerios from $3.99, down to 44 cents per box. That is almost a 90 percent savings! Can you imagine how much you would save and give if you did this every week?

Check Your Store's Policies

Stacking both manufacturer and store coupons is how I grow my stockpile, save money, and am able to give to those in need. And I am able to do it all within a budget of around fifty dollars per week.

You need to double-check your store's policy (see next page), but most retailers will take both store and manufacturer coupons on one product. In my experience, some cashiers don't know this to be the policy, so I simply ask for a customer service manager to verify the policy. I always check the store's policy *before* I get to checkout so I don't cause embarrassment or frustration for myself.

This rule of thumb applies not only to stacking coupons but to the other savings strategies detailed in this book. You need to inquire about these policies at your store's customer service desk before you try them. Knowing the rules ahead of time will save you lots of grief in the checkout line! I highly recommend printing a copy of the store's coupon policy and keeping it with you at all times. This will save you time and hassle if you happen to get an employee who is not familiar with it.

Two Methods of Coupon Organization

To make the most of your manufacturer and store coupons, there are two main methods of coupon organization:

- ◊ clip your coupons and file them away
- ◊ leave your coupons in the inserts, then date and file them

Inserts are the booklets of coupons that come in your Sunday paper, inserted between sales fliers, comics, and the news or are located in the turnstiles at the front of your store. If you label the coupon inserts with the date, you can clip them as they are needed. There are pros and cons to both of these methods. Let's take a look at the advantages, disadvantages, and organization tips below to see which method is for you.

STORE POLICIES CHECKLIST

Here are a few things I find out about a store before I head out to shop

1. Do you have a frequent shopper card for discounts?

2. Do you double or triple coupons? If so, for what amounts?

3. Do you accept printable coupons? Are there any limitations?

4. Does your store provide loadable electronic coupons?

5. Do you price match or take competitors' coupons? If so, from which stores?

6. If you price match, is it the entire ad or just the advertised price for specific items? (For example, Walmart might not honor BOGOF or coupons in store ads, but they'll match specific prices on the same item.)

7. How many "like" coupons will you accept per transaction?

8. When you advertise a product as BOGOF (Buy One Get One Free), are the items marked as 50 percent off each, or is one product at full price and one free?

9. When you advertise a product as 5 for $5, can I buy 1 for $1, or do I have to buy the full amount advertised to receive the discounted price?

10. Do you allow stacking manufacturer and store coupons?

11. Do you have store loyalty programs or incentives for different groups of shoppers, like baby clubs or senior discounts?

12. How does your store handle coupon overages?

Clip and File

"Clip and file" is a method where you take your weekly Sunday coupon inserts and clip all the coupons and file them in a way that suits you best. Check out the advantages and disadvantages below to see if this technique fits your season of life.

Call your local food shelter and ask for a list of items—grocery, toiletries, cleaning supplies—that they need. Then as you clip coupons and read sale ads, buy extras of those items to donate to the food pantry.

Advantages to the Clip and File Method

Clipping every coupon and filing them into some kind of filing system has a few major advantages.

Increase stockpile more quickly. By clipping coupons and having them on hand you will save more money, and you will build up your stockpile much more quickly. That is why I highly recommend this method for beginners. It allows you to build your pantry at a faster rate, therefore saving more money.

The main reason is that you are able to snag all kinds of deals you might have missed when just going through the store ad. Plus, local stores often carry many unadvertised sales that you can't plan for. If I am in the grocery store and I see an unadvertised sale on kids' yogurt, and with a coupon it is free, I will be *very* glad that I had that coupon on hand. Without previously clipping them I would not have been able to grab the deal.

Save on clearance items. If you are at the store and spot a clearance deal that you weren't expecting, you can snag it with your coupon! Clearance deals are unadvertised markdowns that are usually tagged as "manager's specials." They are often on separate rounders (end caps) or shelving systems in the store. Items on clearance are usually marked down by at least 50 percent, so if you use a coupon with a clearance item, you can save big.

Here is an example of the savings power I'm talking about. One day I was shopping at my neighborhood store and discovered they had put laundry detergent on clearance. My store is a neighborhood store, so the shelving space is smaller. This means they make room for new items more often and put items on clearance to make room. I had clipped all my coupons (and multiples of each), and had them all with me. When I looked, I found I had coupons for the sale brand and was able to get ten large bottles of laundry detergent for only five dollars! Even though this item was not on my original shopping list, I try to leave a five- to ten-dollar cushion for any unexpected deals I might find. I was really glad I did that on this particular week!

Here's how: the detergents were clearance priced at $1.50. I had coupons for $1 off. And I had ten coupons for the various brands on clearance, so I got ten bottles of detergent for only 50 cents each!

Laundry Detergents—on clearance for $1.50/ea

$1/1 Laundry Detergent Coupon

Final Price: $.50 each after coupon and clearance sale

Some of you are reading this and thinking, *Why in the world do you need ten bottles of laundry detergent?* In fact, that is what my husband said. I didn't need it all, so I was able to donate some of it to a local food pantry and give some to a friend in need. Also, since laundry detergent is something we always need and it doesn't expire, I can go for the next year without having to purchase laundry detergent. Woot! Woot!

Disadvantages of the Clip and File Method

The clip-and-file method of couponing has a few disadvantages that might lead you to decide on another route. Here are the most common drawbacks to clipping all coupons.

Time-consuming. Clipping multiple coupon inserts each week can be quite time-consuming. Most weekly coupon inserts have quite a few coupons, sometimes a few hundred. Who wants to spend an entire afternoon clipping coupons? You may not mind, but that is just not how I want to spend my time. I no longer clip all my coupons;

I use the "clip as you go" method that I'll describe next. However, if you have kids who can help, clipping coupons is a great task to give your children. Cutting, organizing, and sorting are all good skills they can learn all while helping you out! Remember, not everyone is in the couponing stage or season of life, so don't feel guilty if you aren't able to do this.

. . . .

Start children off on the way they should go, and even
when they are old they will not turn from it.

PROVERBS 22:6

. . . .

LIVING *Generously* TIP

Don't throw out expired coupons; send them to military families. Most overseas military bases accept expired manufacturer's coupons up to six months out. Check out OCPnet.org or CouponsToTroops .com for more details.

Keeping your file updated. Since coupons expire and you have so many, it can be quite a task keeping them up to date. There is nothing worse than planning a shopping trip only to find most of your coupons are expired. You will find most coupons expire at the end of the month and also quarterly. Large quantities of coupons typically expire at the end of March, July, October, and most commonly, December. My tip for updating your coupon file? Much like clipping the coupons, weeding out expired coupons is a great task for your kiddos!

Organizing Your Clipped Coupons

There are many different resources to organize your clipped coupons. You can use a wallet-sized accordion file, a shoebox with envelopes, or even a baseball-card binder with plastic sheet inserts. With many different options available, just find the one that works for you. You are the one who will be using your system, so organize it the way you think it makes sense. Plus, if you decide to clip coupons, you must be intentional at keeping up with it. The disadvantage to clipping all coupons is that it is time-consuming, and honestly, you won't use all the coupons you clip. Getting behind with coupon clipping quickly snowballs into a big job, even if it is neglected for just a couple of weeks!

> *I finished my weekly shopping today. As I was driving into my neighborhood, I had the sinking feeling that I had left my coupon folder in the seat of the shopping cart. I tore through my bags when I got home and sure enough, it was not there. I started crying—hundreds of dollars and hours of clipping: gone. Then customer service at the store called to say they had my coupon folder! Thankfully, I have a label attached to it with my name and phone number, and some wonderful person turned it in for me.*
>
> —*Lora*

Coupon File Categories

When filing my coupons, I like to have the categories as broken down as possible. This makes it much easier to find what I am looking for. Whether you are using a wallet-sized accordion file or baseball card inserts in a three-ring binder, these categories will work for you. (See next page.)

SAVING SAVVY TIP

Put your contact information in your coupon binder so you can retrieve it if you leave it somewhere.

If you use a wallet-sized accordion file, I recommend having two: one for food items and the other for nonfood items.

COMMONLY USED COUPON FILE CATEGORIES

NON-FOOD ITEMS	FOOD ITEMS
Surface/Floor	Beverages
Dishes	Snacks
Laundry	Desserts
Paper/Plastic	Breakfast/Cereal
Teeth	Dairy
Hair	Refrigerated/Yogurt
Medication	Frozen/Canned
Beauty/Makeup	Sauces/Toppings
Soap/Lotion	Meat
Baby	Rice/Pasta/Bread
Deodorant/Shave	Baking
Feminine	Produce
	Miscellaneous

Clip as You Go

The "clip as you go" method is where you take your Sunday coupon inserts and label them with the date on the front, and file them away as whole inserts. You do not clip your coupons in advance; you clip only what you need before you go to the store. Just like the "clip and file" method, "clip as you go" has advantages and disadvantages.

Clipping as you go is a great alternative because of all the online resources available today. On FaithfulProvisions.com, we have a coupon database that catalogs and links to all coupons currently available. You can just look up where the coupon is located, whether it is in an insert, online, or another source, and access it easily. (I'll explain coupon databases in more detail later.)

In clipping as you go, you need to label and date each Sunday insert. I use a permanent marker to date mine, marking boldly on the front cover of the insert before filing it away. You will be able to locate coupons quickly once you learn the coupon lingo. For example, at my website, Faithful Provisions.com, you will see abbreviations that look like this: 9/13 SS or 6/7 RP. This means that the coupon can be found in the September 13 (9/13) Smart Source (SS) insert or the June 7 (6/7) Red Plum (RP) insert. These are inserts that are typically found in your Sunday newspaper.

> *I don't waste my time clipping coupons. I file them by week, wait for you to post the deals, then I only clip the ones I need. I spend about forty-five minutes getting them ready, one hour shopping, and save a ton of money. No tired fingers, no piles of trash, no sorting.*
>
> —Julie

Advantages of the Clip as You Go Method

Saves time. The number one advantage to clipping your coupons as you need them is that you save time. No more long Sunday coupon clipping sessions. You only clip the coupons you need and plan on using. I merely create my list, which indicates where I can find the coupons, and set off to clip only the ones I need. Or if I need a coupon for something in particular, I can just use the Faithful Provisions Coupon Database to quickly find it!

Easy. In addition to saving time, the clip-as-you-go method is so much easier. I don't need to do anything each week except label the date on my insert and drop it into my filing box.

Disadvantages of the Clip as You Go Method

Longer stocking-up period. The greatest challenge most find with this method is that you can't build your stockpile as quickly. You typically aren't as familiar with the coupons you have on hand and by not having them with you at the store, you can't get any "extra" sale items you missed the first time around in the store ad.

Miss out on clearance deals. If you don't have your entire coupon inventory with you, you can't use coupons on unadvertised clearance deals.

Coupon Organization
Systems

Combined Method

I have used both of these methods, but over the last few years I have found that combining these methods works really well for me. I don't have the time or desire to cut all the coupons, but I want to have some on hand with me while I am in the grocery store. So what I do is clip my favorite coupons, or you could even clip one set of inserts, and then I file the rest. The ones I consider my favorites might be items I would purchase without a coupon, or staple items I find I already need to purchase each week, such as almond milk. That way I have some with me in the store, but if I need to do serious stocking up, I will need to plan ahead and come back.

TIP

Remember:
saving savvy
isn't about the
percentage you
save; it is about
learning to save
money overall
so you can live
generously.

How to Organize Coupon Inserts

As with clipping and filing of individual coupons, there are many ways to file the coupon inserts. You can use an 8.5x11 accordion folder, bankers' boxes with file folders, or, my favorite, portable file boxes with a handle and large folder hangers inside. Remember, your system needs to work for you! You know yourself better than anyone, so go with something you find both appealing and doable.

The obvious advantage to clipping as you go is the time-saving factor. I only clip the coupons that I need. This works really well for me because I have a stockpile to pull from and I don't typically "need" a lot of things. I have gotten to a point in my planning that I have almost everything I need to make my meals; I am just on the lookout for the best deals. I don't grab every deal, but I am okay with that. My goal is spending less, not necessarily saving more.

I am of the mind-set that the less time I spend shopping, the more I have of myself to give to my family and to others. Remember this isn't about the percentages you save, or how much you can stock up with a certain amount of money. This is about saving money and living generously. For me it is also about staying within a budget, so you can spend more time with your family and also bless others in the process. Keep it in perspective. Savvy saving is a shift in the way you think about your money, but it is done so that you have more of yourself to give.

Using a Coupon Database

No matter which method of coupon organization you use, a coupon database will help you find coupons for the specific items on your shopping list. Coupon databases are wonderful—as long as you know how to use them! Basically, a coupon database is a searchable online listing of all available coupons. Do some research, and select one that captures the coupons you *want* to use, categorizes the ones you *already have*, and gives you great directions on where the coupons can be found.

Faithful Provisions
Coupon Database

For instance, some databases just say "mailer" as a location, but I want to know which mailer, when it came out, and what it was called. This helps me determine if I already have it and when I got it. The result is much less wasted time on my part. Some of the best databases even include coupons that are found in magazines, and my favorites include links to online coupons that aren't always so easy to find! That is how the Faithful Provisions coupon database works. (See next page for a page view.)

Most coupon databases work like a search engine. I use a coupon database most frequently when I am looking for a specific coupon—especially when I have a "need" item that isn't on sale, and I want to find a coupon to match up with it. Typically you can find a store coupon matchup list, and all you have to do is follow the list.

Here's a scenario: we are out of peanut butter! So I go to an online coupon database, enter "peanut butter" into the database search engine, and within seconds, it displays all the peanut butter coupons that are out there, detailing where to find them, their value, and the expiration dates. I then take the coupons with me when I go shopping and see what brand matches up to get the best deal.

Coupon databases also help you use coupons before they expire; many databases tell you which ones are about to expire. There is nothing I hate worse than to let a coupon expire, especially if it is a staple item I will purchase with or without a coupon. So just searching by expiration date, I can do a quick check and be sure I am not missing any good offers.

Learn to Speak Coupon

At FaithfulProvisions.com and all over the couponing community, you will see many acronyms and terms that will be unfamiliar to you. They may vary from site to site, but this list will help you begin to learn the couponing lingo.

Sunday Paper Inserts

- ◇ **GM**—General Mills insert (Sunday paper); random
- ◇ **P&G**—Proctor & Gamble insert (Sunday paper); monthly
- ◇ **RP**—RedPlum insert (Sunday paper); weekly
- ◇ **SS**—Smart Source insert (Sunday paper); weekly

Drugstore Specific

- **ECB**—Extra Care Bucks; CVS rebate program
- **In-Ad Coupons**—Walgreens weekly ad coupons
- **RR**—Register Rewards; Walgreens "cash" type of coupon for use on a future transaction within expiration period
- **SCR**—Single Check Rebates; RiteAid's monthly rebate program
- **+Up Rewards Program**—Rite Aid's reward program

Coupon Types

- **Blinkie**—A plastic box that dispenses coupons, usually identified by a blinking light, and attached to a store shelf
- **Catalina**—Coupons that print at the register and are returned along with the store receipt. These are usually manufacturer coupons that can be used at any store.
- **IP**—Internet printable coupons
- **Peelie**—A coupon or booklet that is attached to an item and can be "peeled" off immediately to use at point-of-sale or saved for later

Strategy

- **BOGOF / B1G1F**—Buy One Get One Free: On these sales, stores usually allow you to purchase a single item at 50 percent off.
- **Fillers**—Items you add to your purchase to increase your total, usually to be able to use a $x off $xx coupon.
- **WYB**—When You Buy
- **Mfg**—Manufacturer
- **OOP**—Out of Pocket
- **Overages or Moneymakers**—Potential profit after using a coupon with a sale item

- **Rolling**—Roll your money over to the next transaction
- **Stacking**—Using a manufacturer coupon with a store coupon
- **$1/1 or $1/2**—$1 off 1 item, or $1 off 2 items

Coupon Lingo Guide Page

Matching Coupons with Sale Items

There are lots of tools out there to help you match up your coupons with products that are on sale. That is typically the biggest obstacle. So, now that you have all your coupons organized, and you have checked a coupon database to get coupons for items you need, what do you do?

You are in luck, because there are tons of online resources, including my website, FaithfulProvisions.com, that match coupons up with store sale items for you. Yes, we do all the work for you and it is completely free! I don't recommend paying for coupon matchups. There are services available that charge you as little as five dollars per month. But why pay when you can get it for free?

How Does It Work?

Find a website or blog that covers the stores where you shop. They will find coupons that match with store sales or alert you to clear-ance deals, so you don't have to do it yourself. Pick a blog that covers the region in which you live.

Deal Scenario Example

Let's look at a scenario based on my website. The typical layout looks like the example below.

Peter Pan Peanut Butter, 15 oz—$1.50

Use $1/1 Peter Pan Peanut Butter coupon in 12/10 SS insert

Final Price: $.50 after coupon and sale

The scenario will usually list the product, description, and price. Then the post lists all possible coupons available for that product, where to find them, and finally gives you an estimated price. This coupon listing tells you that you can find the $1/1 Peter Pan coupon in your December 10 (12/10) Smart Source (SS) Sunday coupon insert. This is helpful particularly if you do not clip coupons. If you file them using the "clip as you go" method, you can go to your coupon inserts filed by date, and easily pull and clip the coupon to take on your shopping trip. Remember, prices vary by region, but the Faithful Provisions posts will usually give you a pretty good idea of what you can expect to pay for the item at that store.

Doubling and Tripling Coupons

Many grocery stores will double and even triple coupons. Lots of people ask me, "What do I need to do to get my coupons to double?" The answer is nothing! Most stores that offer double or triple couponing only require you to swipe your store loyalty card.

Here is how your checkout experience would look at a store that doubles up to 50 cents every day.

1. Scan your loyalty card (if the store has one).
2. Scan all items you are purchasing.
3. Once you are given a total, hand all coupons to cashier.
4. As the cashier is scanning coupons, the receipt will first say "vendor coupon" or something similar, and then underneath, it will note some wording like "multiplied coupon," looking like this:

    Vendor Coupon ....−$0.50
    Multiplied Coupon..............................−$0.50
    That equals a total of $1 off, just for using that one coupon!

Knowing you can use one manufacturer coupon per item, check out this deal scenario: If you find spaghetti sauce on sale for $1.50 and you have a manufacturer coupon from the Sunday paper for 40 cents off one jar of spaghetti sauce, you can get that spaghetti sauce for only 70 cents if your store doubles your coupon. If you have more than one (of the same) coupon, you can get as many jars of sauce for this rock-bottom price as you have coupons. This is one of the best ways to quickly build your stockpile!

Prego Spaghetti Sauce, 32 oz jar—$1.50

$0.40/1 Prego Spaghetti Sauce coupon

Final Price: $.70 per jar after sale and doubled coupon

Coupon Overage or Moneymakers

As you grow in your knowledge and skills of coupon usage you will begin to notice that sometimes a coupon discount is more than the actual cost of the item. In some instances, this can lead to what couponers call "overages" or a "moneymaker" situation. Each store is different as to how they handle this. Some stores reduce the value of the coupon manually at the register, some have a computer system that catches it automatically, and some stores allow for coupon overage.

Read the comments that other readers leave on blog posts to find additional deal tips or coupon matchups.

Note that if you shop at a store that allows overages, you will not be paid to take products home! So be sure to calculate what is in your cart. If you find yourself in a coupon overage situation, add something else to your cart to account for the difference.

Coupon Clipping Services

A popular way you can get a coupon without purchasing multiple papers or if you forgot to purchase that week's newspaper is by using a coupon clipping service. This is another great way to save while collecting more coupons.

How They Work

Coupon clipping services do not sell coupons. Selling coupons is not authorized by the manufacturers and is illegal. Instead, coupon clipping services charge for the service of collecting, cutting, sorting, and filing the coupons. Then you pay the shipping and handling costs, which can be as low as the cost of a stamp.

Some of the popular Coupon Clipping Services are sites like:

◇ TheCouponClippers.com

◇ TheCouponMaster.com

◇ CouponsThingsbyDede.com

You need to be careful where you are purchasing your coupons to make sure the service is legitimate. Because sites like eBay set the price of the coupon by its popularity, it can turn into a bidding war and in essence is a charge for the actual coupon, which is illegal.

Using a coupon clipping service requires more advance planning. For instance, you need to purchase your coupons a few days before the sale ad for that store even comes out. So, if you want a coupon for a CVS deal for the sale ad that comes out on Sunday, you would have to purchase the coupons for that deal by the Friday before. This way you have enough time to have them mailed so you can use them before the sale ad runs out.

When using a service, know that you can't purchase just one coupon. You must purchase a minimum dollar amount, either by ordering multiples of one coupon, an insert, or mix and match different coupons.

Pros of Coupon Clipping Services

One of the benefits of using a coupon clipping service is if there's a coupon you see on other regional blogs, you can typically get them by ordering them. I've found that sometimes you have to look at a few different coupon clipping services, because if one of them is in your region, they won't have that particular coupon either.

Another benefit is if there is one particular coupon you want, you can pay a dime for it instead of the dollar or more to buy another paper. So on things that my family *really* wants, I can buy multiple coupons to get multiple items while they are on sale and really stock up!

Cons of Coupon Clipping Services

The downside of using coupon clipping services is that you have to order the coupons the day you see the sale ad. For example, if something is on sale and your store's ad comes out on Wednesday, you need to order your coupons that day. Hopefully you'd get them by Monday, so you would still have a few days to shop. If you wait until Thursday or Friday to order your coupons, it could be Wednesday before you get them and possibly too late to use them. It's a little bit of a risk.

The best time I've had using a service is when I can forecast a deal at a store ahead of time. And sometimes stores like Walgreen's or CVS run a monthly deal on a particular item, so you have more time to order the coupon.

Host a Coupon Swap

A coupon swap is a great way to find coupons you need and provide others with coupons you may not use. These can be fun, social get-togethers where you encourage each other and share information. You can easily get more of the coupons that you are most interested in and help someone else at the same time by swapping the ones you will not use. For example, a mom of teenage girls would be willing to swap coupons for diapers and juice boxes with a mother of toddlers who is willing to trade her coupons for beauty and skin care items.

You can also share couponing ideas and tips with others at a coupon swap. You might have found a great deal on a product or even know about a store policy change that you want to share. A coupon swap is a great place to do this.

To organize and hold a successful coupon swap, here are a few tips to make it run smoothly:

- *Plan ahead.* The key to coupon swaps is to promote them in advance and set them up to occur regularly. For instance, you could set it up to be the last Thursday night of each month. This helps everyone anticipate and plan for a great swap!

- *Allow plenty of time.* You will need a two- to three-hour time slot to effectively get through your coupons. I suggest an evening or weekend, unless you have moms who can meet during the school day and turn it into a potluck lunch.

- *Know who's there.* A great way to get to know everyone is to supply name tags.

- *Collect expired coupons.* Collect expired coupons for military personnel and designate one person to be in charge each month to mail them to the appropriate contact. See OCPnet.org or Coupons ToTroops.com for more information.

- *Donate extra items.* Provide a donation drop box for surplus food and toiletries purchased with coupons. This is an easy way to donate because you don't have to make a separate trip to drop off your goods. Just pick one person per month, or call a local food pantry and see if they are willing to show up and take the items for you.

- *Set the mood.* Play some fun music and turn it into a girls' night out by having everyone bring a dish—make it a potluck.

- *Provide supplies.* Have the following supplies on hand: scissors, permanent markers/pens, envelopes, trash can.

Do Stores and Manufacturers Lose Money on Coupons?

Here is a question I get about couponing on my blog and in the workshops I teach: "How do the stores and manufacturers make any money if we are using all these coupons?"

If you believe that stores and manufacturers are losing money on coupons, then be warned: it is a myth.

- ◇ Stores do not run promotions if they aren't going to make any money on them.
- ◇ Manufacturers do not offer promotions if they aren't going to make any money on them.

If coupons are used properly and we consumers follow the manufacturer and store rules on using coupons, everyone wins! By using coupons, you are taking advantage of the resources that stores and manufacturers offer, and you are maneuvering your own shopping habits in order to make the most of the savings. With a little extra effort, you can find some great deals to save you thousands of dollars over the course of your lifetime.

Life Cycle of a Manufacturer Coupon

Every coupon that is accepted by a retail store is returned to the store as money in the form of a check from that manufacturer.

Here is how it works:

1. Manufacturer or store runs a coupon promotion.
2. You use the coupon at your store.
3. The store collects all coupons redeemed and sends them to a clearing house to tally.
4. The coupons are scanned and then sorted by manufacturer.

5. An invoice and the coupons are sent to each manufacturer for the coupons collected for that store.

6. The manufacturer cuts a check to the store for the redeemed coupons.[2]

How Store Coupons Work

SAVING SAVVY TIP

Catalina coupons (the register tape that comes out with your receipt) are typically manufacturer coupons, not just for a store. Even though they say, "Redeemable at (store name)," they may be used at any store that accepts manufacturer coupons.

Earlier, I covered what a store coupon is; now let's look at how they work. Store coupons are a discount extended through the store. The store receives many different incentives to promote particular manufacturer products through the store coupon programs.

Advertising Fee

Manufacturers pay an advertising fee to have a store coupon or sale notice placed in the store ad or store coupon flyers. This is why you sometimes see items in a sale ad that aren't really on sale. The manufacturer might have purchased an ad slot to promote its product in the store sales flyers. That is why you need to use tools like the free Provisions Price List iPhone app or Provisions Price List downloadable PDF, so you can determine what is really on sale, and what is just an ad placed in the sales circular.

Discounted Products

Stores get massive discounts to promote a product. The store will have a contract with the manufacturer to purchase a certain amount of a product for a deep discount. Instead of offering the product on the shelves as a sale for everyone, they store decides to run it as a "store coupon." So only those who use the coupon get the discount.

This is a huge moneymaker for stores. They got the item at a deep discount, and only those who use the coupon get a discount on the item that they are making a nice profit on! Therefore, their profit on non-coupon-using shoppers far outweighs any money they didn't make off you. Remember, stores are always making a profit somewhere! If they weren't, they wouldn't present these programs.

An example of this is:

1. A store purchases 1,000 Kraft shredded cheese products for 25 cents per bag.
2. They sell the cheese at $2.00 per bag and offer a store coupon for $1 off per bag.

If 800 customers purchase a bag of cheese at full price (which is still a good deal), and 200 purchase it at $1 per bag, the store only had a $250 investment in the program. They make $1,500 for running the program (which is a huge profit of 600 percent). The store didn't lose any money, and the consumer still got a great deal on cheese!

Store-brand items still make a profit. The markup on the store-brand items is huge because the stores get such a good deal on it, so even if you use a store coupon on their brand item, both you and the store are doing well.

Ethics and Etiquette of Couponing

In his book *There's No Such Thing as "Business" Ethics*, well-known speaker and author John C. Maxwell states that "ethics is never a business issue or a social issue or a political issue. It is a personal issue."[3] He goes on to say that we should remember the golden rule and think about "How would I like to be treated in this situation?"

Believe it or not, this applies to couponing. It saddens me to hear about unethical and fraudulent coupon usage. Consider a situation that happened in my community recently and hurt many local couponers.

A shopper went to a local store with a competitor's printable coupon and bought more than ninety bags of trail mix! The shopper had made photocopies of the printable coupon and the cashier accepted them. These coupons were meant to be one print per computer, and photocopying them is coupon fraud. This shopper's abuse of the system (and others like this person) hinders the rest of us who do follow the rules. When something like this happens, store policies can change within a matter of days. In my area, several restrictions concerning the use of competitors' coupons were quickly put in place. Bottom line: it only takes a few bad apples to spoil the bunch. Because of this shopper's actions, I was prohibited from using my printable coupon for any item.

Now, as I point you toward honest and ethical couponing with the following guidelines, I concede that even with the best of intentions, I do sometimes make mistakes. Know that my goal here and on FaithfulProvisions.com is to provide ethical ways to use coupons. I try very hard to make sure all my links and deal matchups are in accordance with store and manufacturer policies. If you ever find one that I have laid out incorrectly, please let me know as quickly as possible!

No Photocopying

This should go without saying, but I am compelled to make sure there is no ambiguity. All coupons, especially online coupons, are not to be photocopied. Most have a special number that allows the manufacturer to track the number of coupons issued and see how many were actually redeemed.

In addition, most of the time, if you photocopy a coupon and try to use it at the register, only one will work. The rest will not scan because the computer has already noted that number. So, even if your printer jams and you lose your coupon, you should not photocopy a coupon. I know, it stinks when that happens, but you are committing an illegal activity by photocopying a coupon. There are only a certain number of prints allowed per coupon.

Beware of PDF Coupons

A rule of thumb regarding PDF files for printable coupons is that these are usually fraudulent unless they are found on the official manufacturer or store website. If the coupon looks too good to be true, has no expiration date, and is free, chances are it is bogus.

Fraudulent Coupons

If you spot a fraudulent coupon, submit it to the Coupon Information Center (CIC) at couponinformationcenter.com. In their efforts to combat coupon fraud, they keep a list of those that have been identified as fraudulent by the manufacturers. They also work closely with manufacturers and retailers to advocate for appropriate use of coupons. If you are ever in doubt, remember this resource and check their list to verify the validity of your coupons.

- *Too-good-to-be-true is usually false.* If a coupon seems too good to be true, it probably is. Coupons that offer items for free that can be printed from your home computer should set off a red flag, unless you can verify that the coupon can be found on the manufacturer website.

- *Be wary of paying for free coupons.* Why would you pay for a free item coupon? If someone is trying to sell free coupons and you know the coupons didn't come from a newspaper insert, be wary.

- *Beware of multiple coupons.* If a seller has more than one free item coupon on sale and is selling multiples of it, be concerned. Not only is it rare that one person will have multiples of the same free item coupon, but they are usually mailed directly to the consumer from the manufacturer and almost always have a watermark or hologram on them to prevent copying—which is coupon fraud.

- *E-mail the seller.* Send an e-mail to the seller and confirm that the coupon was mailed to them directly from the manufacturer. If they can't or won't verify this information, do not proceed with this seller.

- ◇ *Double-check it.* If you don't see your printable coupon listed on the CIC website, double-check it against HotCouponWorld.com's forum "It's Got to Be Real."[4] They keep track of and identify questionable coupons.

- ◇ *Trash it.* If you learn that you have a fraudulent coupon, play it safe and throw it away.

Expired Coupons

I used expired coupons in the beginning of my coupon journey, until I realized it was not an appropriate practice. Even then, I continued justifying my practice because I knew the stores would get reimbursed anyway, but sin is a slippery slope, isn't it? Even knowing they would get reimbursed wasn't going to cut it. I was not following the store policies set out for me and the Lord let me know it. I had an uneasy feeling every time I used them. But the Lord quickly showed me I could use coupons by the rules and still save big!

One thing I have learned is that these deals and coupons are put out for a reason, and we should try to use them for their intended purpose—hence the expiration dates. Although I have heard tons of stories on the coupon redemption process, including when and how stores get reimbursed, I promote proper coupon usage, which means I do not endorse the use of expired coupons. (The one exception to this case is the military and I will cover that in chapter 9.)

LIVING *Generously* TIP

If you are in a store and realize you don't need specific coupons, be a "coupon angel" and leave the coupons on top of products for others to use.

Keep All Coupons

Don't throw away a coupon unless you wouldn't want the item for free or you wouldn't be willing to give the free item to someone else. Coupons are a great way to be able to give items to others through food pantries, women's shelters, and homeless missions. You can also create food baskets for families you know who are in need.

Another reason to keep all coupons is the opportunity to share your coupons with others. If you don't end up using a coupon, you can be one of the "coupon angels" who leave valuable coupons at stores for others to use.

> " I had read about the "coupon angels," shoppers who leave valuable coupons lying around in stores, and it was something I had been meaning to do. Today I stopped at CVS to get some nearly-free Glade products, only to discover that I left my $4 Sense and Spray coupons at home. Well, I looked at a Sense and Spray on the shelf, and what did I see on top of the box? One of the $4 coupons! Needless to say, I used it to purchase the item for pennies. Whoever left that coupon, thank you. I can't wait to do for others what you did for me. "
>
> —James

Remember, even when coupons are expired, military families can use them! Check out chapter 9 for more ways to give back.

Is couponing beginning to make sense to you? If you decided to use this method to stock up, enabling you to not only save money but also to donate valuable items to those less fortunate, don't you think this would change your life? It would change the lives of countless others, as well.

DO'S AND DON'TS OF COUPONING

DO NOT . . .	DO . . .
1. Use expired coupons	1. Stack a store coupon and a manufacturer coupon for greater savings.
2. Photocopy coupons.	2. Stock ahead by obtaining multiple coupon inserts from more than one newspaper.
3. Use fraudulent coupons.	3. Use a coupon database to find and catch coupons about to expire.

SAVINGS STRATEGIES FOR
COUPONING

IF YOU HAVE *MORE* TIME . . .

1. **Clip and file coupons.** Having more time will allow you to save more by clipping all coupons and filing them so you can take them to the store to grab missed sale and clearance items.

2. **Stack manufacturer and store coupons.** When an item is on sale, stack a manufacturer coupon with a store coupon to save the most.

3. **Host a coupon swap.** A great way to get extra coupons for free and donate your unused ones is to either attend or host a coupon swap in your area.

4. **Use a coupon clipping service.** If you are out of time, or want to stock up on a particular item, use a coupon clipping service to get more coupons for the items you want.

5. **Read blog comments.** When you are on a blog that does coupon matchups or deals, be sure to read through the readers' comments. There are usually lots of gems found in there!

IF YOU HAVE *LESS* TIME . . .

1. **Buy store brands.** If you can't find a coupon to go with a sale item, sometimes you are better off just purchasing the store brand.

2. **Use coupons for sale items.** The best way to use coupons is in conjunction with a sale item.

3. **Use a coupon database.** Use a coupon database to easily and quickly find the coupons you are looking for either online, in Sunday coupon inserts, or in coupon booklets.

4. **File coupons by insert.** If you are looking to save time, file your Sunday coupon inserts and booklets by date or topic. Then use the coupon database to easily find them.

5. **Know store policies.** Before heading to your store, make sure you know their policies on things like BOGOF items and doubling coupons. This prevents a lot of stress at the checkout lane.

6. **Learn coupon lingo.** One of the most important things to know are the abbreviations you will see on blogs and coupon matchup sites. Print the list off and keep it handy, no memorizing needed!

Chapter 6
. . . .

GROCERY SHOPPING PREPARATION

If you have read the chapters up to this point, you are well on your way to a new life-style of saving money and living generously. For instance, you have:

- ◇ figured out why it is important to your family to save and give
- ◇ stocked up your pantry and put food in the freezer
- ◇ learned how to plan your meals
- ◇ decided whether to use coupons for additional savings

In this chapter I will prepare you to make a detailed plan for your shopping trip with the new mindset: never pay full price for anything.

Now comes the time when you take all the skills you have developed and turn them into habit. Not just any habit, mind you, but a productive, fruitful habit that will be a blessing to your family. This is where you will save money while you shop. Being prepared for the grocery trip is built upon everything you have learned so far. The space you created to stock up on items for the pantry and freezer, the meal planning, the recognition of staple items and "go-to" meals, the coupon clipping and organizing, reading the grocery store sale ads—all of that leads to the grocery store itself.

Just as you plan your meals, you will benefit greatly when you plan your trips to the store. Why? If you don't plan for the grocery trip, you're going to:

- ◇ spend more
- ◇ save less
- ◇ waste a lot of time *and* money

That doesn't sound like a formula for success to me. So, before you run out the door to replenish the pantry, freezer, and refrigerator, slow down and think it through. Ask yourself these questions:

- ◇ What is my budget (how much can we afford to spend on food)?
- ◇ What is on sale this week?
- ◇ What do we need?
- ◇ What do we already have on hand?

This is going to require some discipline.

- ◇ You will need to commit to a few things, such as not buying impulse items or shopping on an empty stomach.
- ◇ You will need to commit to a shopping plan and choose a day of the week to hit the store.
- ◇ You'll need to know what your family eats and what your calendar looks like.

This process sounds structured, but it will save you money and time. Remember, I want to encourage you and help you along this savings journey. My goal is to show you how to shop smart and be savvy about your saving strategies. You can do it!

The condition of family economics is a continuing concern, especially today. I know several moms who would like to find a part-time job, especially if it was something they could do from home. What if you considered learning and implementing this new way of shopping as your part-time job? Then, I'll bet you could find time for it. Would you accept a job working from home, at your convenience, if it paid for half of what you are currently spending on groceries? Sure you would! So consider yourself hired. The little bit of planning you are going to incorporate into your schedule will make all the difference in your ability to save money and run your household more smoothly. Are you ready? Let's get to work!

Set Your Grocery Budget

Let's start your grocery plan at the beginning: your budget. What is your grocery budget? A grocery budget is simply how much money you have to spend each month on groceries.

Track your spending. If you don't know your monthly grocery budget, I suggest looking back at your last two to three months of expenses and totaling what you spent per month on all your food, toiletries, paper products, and cleaning items. Just look at your bank statements and quickly add up how much you spent each month. It doesn't have to be to the penny. The goal is to get a ballpark amount. Why? If you don't know what you are spending, you will have no clue what you are saving. I recommend that you have a realistic amount to start with so you can track your savings!

Set a grocery budget to start tracking your savings.

Set a monthly grocery budget. Now that you know what you have been spending, this will serve as your grocery budget for now. If that is what you have been spending, then you have inadvertently been budgeting for that amount each month. You may not have known it, but you have a budget! So, for now, you will stick with it. Just writing down that dollar amount on paper gives you a starting point. This is your beginning budget!

. . . .

Suppose one of you wants to build a tower. Won't
you first sit down and estimate the cost to see if
you have enough money to complete it?

LUKE 14:28

. . . .

A Few More Words about the Budget

I know what some of you are thinking: *I don't want to budget! It is so limiting!* But honestly, there is nothing better than knowing exactly where you stand financially each month. If the word *budget* bothers you, then call it a spending plan. If you don't have a budget, you don't have a plan for your money.

Face it, your money is going somewhere, with or without any planning from you. Wouldn't you rather tell your money where to go, than to notice at month's end that, like Elvis, it has left the building? Before I started my saving savvy lifestyle, my husband and I checked our bank statements and tallied the amount of money we spent on groceries and eating out—and we were floored to realize we were spending close to $1,100 per month. That's when it was just the two of us! If your total leaves you feeling as shocked as we were, then you should know that even the smallest improvements will feel great and make a major impact.

> **"** *My husband and I have been budgeting since we were first married, and let me tell you, it has cut down on our money fights. When we want to buy something, we always say, "Put it on the budget!" Budgeting monthly has helped us stretch our dollars, and even more importantly, it keeps communication open in our marriage.* **"**
>
> —Caroline

Now that you have learned what your grocery budget is, you can focus on how to maximize the money you have to spend. I think this is one of the greatest challenges in the saving savvy lifestyle. Sometimes it is hard to stay within your budget when you are aiming to prepare nutritious meals, striving to give generously to food ministries, and attempting to include some fun food items for your family. So, let's look at some ways you can effectively maximize your budget and stretch your grocery dollars.

Determine a Grocery Planning Day

One of the helpful things I started doing early on was to determine a grocery planning day each week. Mine is Friday. I like to have my next week of meals and shopping planned out before the weekend so I can enjoy family time and take my much-needed day of rest on the weekend. You can pick any day of the week that works with your schedule; just be sure to pick one! I believe it is very important to take a day of rest each week. By planning ahead you can relax and enjoy the fruits of your labor. That is what God did, and He commands us to do it too.

. . . .

For in six days the Lord made the heavens and the earth, the sea, and all that is in them, but he rested on the seventh day.

EXODUS 20:11

. . . .

Planning is the most time-consuming part of your grocery store trip. You see, all the work should be done *before* you ever set foot in the grocery store. Truly, this is where the savings really happen. Even if you are organized by nature, the grocery planning process might be a challenge for you! However, I believe that while planning can be the most challenging piece of this puzzle, it is by far the most rewarding.

A New Habit

When you have your grocery budget established, you are on your way to changing your buying habits so that you are learning how to stock ahead and buy the items you always get when they are at their lowest price. Don't look at changing your buying totals yet. We will address reducing your budget later. Right now you just need to determine your spending habits so you can put a plan together for where you want to be on your budget in the future.

The goal right now is to have some structure—that budget number—to work within each week. So take that monthly amount that you have been spending and break it down into what is now your weekly grocery budget. This is what you will stick with for the next four to six weeks while you are stocking up.

Once you learn this new way of shopping, your total food expense will be easily reduced. Start dreaming about what you will do with all the money you are going to save!

Start with What You Already Have

Before you start making your shopping list based on your meal plan, take a look at what you already have available. Check your pantry, refrigerator, and freezer. By doing this you are creating a little extra cushion in your budget for those sale items you want to stock up on. Grab your freezer inventory sheet, look in your pantry, and see what you have. Using what you have is always the best place to start.

As we discussed in the meal planning chapter, I plan my meals around two things: the items I already have on hand and the deals I find each week at the grocery store. My goal is to write my meal plan while I am doing my grocery planning.

Make a Shopping List

Recently I was traveling across Middle Tennessee to teach a workshop in an unfamiliar area. I had a map and directions, but as I drove I decided to catch up on some phone calls, and before I knew it, I got distracted, missed a turn, and I was lost! Eventually I found my way back to the right road and reached my destination. But I wasted a lot of time, arrived later than I planned, and was flustered and frustrated.

To save time, write your weekly meal plan while you are preparing your grocery list.

Like a road map, your shopping list is the plan that will help you reach your destination: saving money! It's easy to veer off this written plan when you see something that looks interesting, you get caught up talking with friends, or something else distracts you. You can get off the right track and end up flustered and frustrated, miles away from your intended destination.

I seldom veer from my shopping list when I have taken the time to prepare it. I have worked hard, creating my meal plan from what I have on hand and knowing exactly what I need to purchase, with a small cushion set aside for any clearance deals I might find. Because I try not to add one more layer of anxiety or stress to my already busy life, I choose to trust my shopping list.

. . . .

Jesus said to his disciples: "Therefore I tell you, do not worry about your life, what you will eat; or about your body, what you will wear. For life is more than food, and the body more than clothes."

LUKE 12:22-23

. . . .

Sale Ads and How to Read Them

On your next grocery trip, pick up the sale ad at your store or save one from your local paper. They are usually in a basket close to the entrance or at the customer service desk. The weekly sale ads are a very important tool when saving money. They are the key to knowing what to buy and when to get it. The sale ads let you know what is on sale each week in the store.

Learning to decipher these sale ads is a very important piece of this puzzle. There are terms you are familiar with, but you may not know exactly what they mean. I, too, had to learn how to speak the language of sale ads. The good news is it is easy to pick up and you'll be a pro in no time.

By using the sale ads to shop and plan your meals, you can save 30 to 50 percent each week.

These days every major grocery store posts their weekly sale ads online. So even if you don't have a newspaper to get the physical ad, or you can't drop by the store, you can look it up online. This allows you to plan your trip before you get to the store.

Using a sale ad is your entry point to saving money. This is your home base, the place you go if all else fails. Shop and plan your meals according to what is on sale. Using the store's weekly sale ad to shop and plan your meals will save you at least 30 to 50 percent each week.

Deciphering the nuances of the sale ad is an entirely different story. In order to plan properly, you need to know how to read one. Yes, it is an art form!

Sale Ad Dates

Sale ad dates, or "run dates," are crucial. These are the dates the sale prices and special offers are effective. While stores vary their start and end dates, sales typically either start on Sunday and end on Saturday, or they start on Wednesday and end the following Tuesday. I know you are thinking, *Why is this such a big deal?* Well, let me explain.

If I were to pull together my shopping list on Friday for a grocery store whose sales ad runs Sunday to Saturday, and I don't get to the store until Sunday, guess what? Everything I planned to purchase from the ad I used on Friday is no longer on sale. Sunday starts the new sale ad, and thus, the new sale prices. So all my planning was in vain. I actually did this one time, but never again. I had to turn around and go home because I was completely unprepared. It did make me stop and remember, *I actually used to grocery shop this way!*

Types of Store Sales

Stores promotions vary, but the two most common ones seem to be:

⋄ Buy One Get One Free—BOGO, B1G1F, or BOGOF

⋄ X for $X—usually something like 10 for $10 or 2/$5

Most large grocery store chains will let you purchase a single BOGOF item at half price. Drugstores, big box stores, and smaller or specialty stores typically do not. Check with your store's customer service department to verify this, though. With the X for $X sale, you can usually purchase just one of an item and still get the sale price. For instance, if your store runs a sale where you buy 10 cans of green beans for $10, you can usually purchase just one can for $1. It is also typically the case with the BOGOF sales. If cereal is on sale BOGOF, and it is usually $4, you can purchase just one box for $2, instead of having to purchase two for $4. But again, be sure to check your store's policy on BOGOF items.

Loss Leaders

Loss leaders are items that are put out at a deep discount for the sake of offering another product or service at a greater profit to attract new customers. The price can even be so low that the product is sold at a loss. A loss leader is often a popular item.

A good example of this is razor blades. Companies like Gillette essentially give their razor units away for free, knowing that customers will have to buy their replacement blades, which is where this type of product typically makes its profit.

Loss leaders are items that people usually purchase on a weekly basis, like milk or bread, and that draw customers into the store to purchase additional items. The store might not make a profit or might take a loss on the item, but they more than make up for it in the other offerings that are highly marked up.

Ad Placements

Just because an item is colorfully displayed on the front page of a store's sales ad doesn't mean it's a good deal. To save money, you must be an educated consumer. Manufacturers often purchase ad space in the sale ads to feature their products, and these ads may

When reading sale ads, know your prices because many items in the ad are not actually a good deal.

not reflect a discount or sale price. While an item may say "low price," it may actually be the regular price. Its spot in the sale ad could have been purchased by the manufacturer in order to push the product. This is a common marketing tactic used by both retailers and manufacturers to sell products at regular price. This is where your price list really comes in handy. When you are wondering, *Is it really a good price?* Check your price list. Maybe it is a good deal or maybe it is just an ad. (See page 22 to download the Provisions iPhone app or Provisions Price List.)

Match Shopping Items to Store Sales and Coupons

As we discussed in chapter 5, the best way to save money is to be strategic in your couponing. The easiest and best way to do that is to only use a coupon with an item that is on sale. The best part is that you don't have to do the work yourself. Instead of spending hours scanning the store circulars and finding coupons to go with the items you need, FaithfulProvisions.com (as well as many other blogs) have already done the work for you . . . completely free! As I mentioned earlier, there is no need to pay for a service to match coupons with store sale items because of the information available for free on the Internet. In fact, many of the free websites not only have much better content but are more personable, giving you ideas on how to use these items you find on sale.

Buy Your Needs First

When you begin, you will notice your shopping list will have two categories: "needs" and "stock-up" items. Each week you have to get your needs, and these items aren't necessarily a good deal, but you need them on a frequent basis. Items can include things such as milk, eggs, and fresh produce. When I do my grocery planning, I begin here. That way, I know how much I have left to work with if I want to do any stocking ahead. Sometimes, this means I may have to go to more than one store in order to get the best deal each week. However, because I have done the prep work at home and I have planned my purchases, I know where I'm going and why. This takes the guesswork out of the equation. You'll find that planning not only saves you money, but it saves you time and cuts down on waste because you are shopping on purpose. My grocery trips are pretty much in and out (frequently under thirty minutes)—nothing like the one-and-a-half-hour sessions I used to endure!

To help you maximize your grocery trips, consider making a shopping list template of your most commonly purchased items. I have provided a Grocery Shopping List as a free download on FaithfulProvisions.com that you can adapt for your own preferences. My shopping list template is arranged by categories, so I can see everything I need in each section of the store without having to backtrack to get missed items.

Grocery Shopping
List Template

Once I have listed my necessities, then I focus on what is on sale and what I want to stock up on. You'll find that once you have been stocking up for a while, you will have enough on hand to do your weekly meal planning. Eventually, your grocery trip will look like mine. You'll purchase your perishables—dairy and fresh produce—and use the rest of your budget to stock up on sale items.

No matter what your monthly budget, get anything you can get for free with coupons matched with sale ads. You can donate the free items to a food pantry, shelter, or someone in need.

Stocking up can lead to another issue: how do you determine what you will get when there are so many good deals? Unfortunately, living on a budget means you will have to turn down some of those good deals, but saying no can be a good thing. I usually start with the staples and grab the best deals in meats. Meats are the most expensive part of my budgeting and meal planning. Since they freeze well, it is easy to go ahead and stock up on them. You need to determine what your "budget busters" are and start there. With the money I have remaining, I include other good deals that I want or like but that are not necessarily priorities. For example, the other day, my grocery store had a sale on a five-pound bag of flour for 88 cents. I do a lot of baking and it is a great donation item, so I purchased ten bags. That gives me several to freeze and a couple to give away.

Then of course, I get anything I can get for free. Even if I don't need it, I can donate it.

Paper-Clip Coupons to Your List

When I am teaching a class, I have two stories I tell as reminders of why you should paper-clip the coupons you are using to your grocery list or put them in an envelope and paper clip that to your list.

First, when I was new to couponing, I developed a bad habit of just tucking my coupons into the fold of my shopping list. One day at the store, I realized that I had accidentally turned the list upside-down, and there was a trail of coupons behind me! Thankfully, I noticed them before I had gotten too far. I was able to find them all, but as falling paper will do, they had floated and scattered under shelves and other carts.

My friend Mandy was not so lucky. I got a call from her one day and when I answered the phone, she sounded upset. She had just started couponing and was making her first big shopping trip. It was raining, and after dashing from her car to the grocery doorway, she looked back to realize that all her coupons had fallen onto the wet ground. Have you ever tried to pick up thin, wet paper off a parking lot surface in the rain? Needless to say, they were all ruined.

The moral of these stories is to avoid losing your coupons by clipping them to your shopping list!

Find a Grocery Buddy

I highly recommend finding a "grocery buddy." Your buddy should be someone who is as interested in saving money as you are. It can be someone in your season of life to help you find deals you missed, or someone at a different season who can give you coupons and deals for things they don't need. You two will commit to encourage and help each other save as much money as possible! For instance, a friend of mine knew I loved the organic produce that is sold at a store that is kind of far for me to drive. So when she was in that area, she would pick up items for me.

For those of you with a competitive spirit, find a friend who makes it fun to see "how low you can go." This is a fun game where you see who can get their grocery budget the lowest while getting the items your family needs. My friends Rebecca and Beth compare notes each week after their shopping trips to keep each other motivated! Besides enjoying the brag session as they share the deals they snagged, they are also eager to help each other continue to spend less!

" *My friend Amy got me started with coupons, and she was the first to point me to your site! She emails me whenever she sees a deal that she knows a fellow mother of young kiddos would appreciate (like apple juice). Then my friend Wendy got started with couponing. She has six children and clips eight papers' worth of coupons every week! She loves it! She keeps me encouraged to do my four papers' worth every week.* "

—Rachel

" *My husband wanted to support me in doing this, so he's my grocery buddy right now . . . and I love that! At home he cuts coupons, then he pulls coupons while I put the list together. He goes to the store with me and helps to make sure that we're getting the right products. He never complains and is always cheering me on with the savings. What an encouragement!* "

—Jenifer

" *I have a couple of friends who keep me motivated when I don't want to hunt down all the deals. All they have to do is text me with their great deals and I am ready to go! It is really great to have that support!* "

—Jessica

. . . .

Two are better than one, because they have
a good return for their labor.

ECCLESIASTES 4:9

. . . .

Use a Grocery Budget List

Your grocery budget list is your shopping list with an added feature: an idea of what you should be paying. Have you ever visited the grocery store with your list, shopped, and paid only to leave scratching your head because you spent too much? Well, that is what I used to do. Having not only a list, but an itemized list of what I'm purchasing and what my totals should be, sets me so much more at ease. Because I know what I should be spending, I am immediately aware of any overcharges when I'm checking out. This can turn into real savings.

Let the savings serve as your incentive to write down all your planned purchases, then, add up the total so you know at checkout what you should be paying. (Don't forget to include any state taxes that apply!)

Page 139 shows how you can set up your grocery budget list. Go to FaithfulProvisions.com and download the free Weekly Grocery Budget List as your template or photocopy the one in the back of this book. Or if you create your own, you'll need three columns. (List each store separately if you go to more than one.)

Grocery Budget List Template

Quantity

The first column should contain the quantity of the item you are going to purchase. If it is an item for which you have a coupon, the number of coupons you have usually determines how many you will purchase. If it is meat or produce, I go by how much money I have to work with and how much my family relies on it for our favorite meals.

Deal Scenario

In the next column, list the item and a detailed description of the type and size that is on sale. Once I included jelly on my list, only to find that the one the store was advertising at a sale price was a particular size and only one flavor. Since I wasn't planning on purchasing that flavor, I would have been perplexed at the checkout if I hadn't noticed that little detail while doing my planning.

Total

The last column should tally the total cost of that item. Simply multiply the quantity times the purchasing price (with your already deducted coupon savings). This method is especially helpful when you are purchasing meat, because $1.99 per pound seems fairly inexpensive until you buy ten pounds of it!

Now that you have an itemized list, calculate what the entire trip should cost and put it at the top of the page. This way, at payment time you will not be surprised by what your spending total is.

The Biggest Difference

One of the greatest lessons I have learned through this saving savvy journey is that I need the Lord in it. I need Him to guide me. I need to follow Him. But before I could follow Him wholeheartedly, I had to give up all the things I thought I needed or how I should do it and submit instead to His plans for me. After all, He made me and created me for His glory, to fulfill His will for my life. His plan is the ultimate one for me; any plan I could conceive on my own pales in comparison. If I know this is true, then why would I ever want to follow my own plan? The answer is because I am sinful, human, and selfish.

God gently showed me that I needed to change my heart to reflect what He wanted for me. He showed me that the things I thought I needed did not compare to what He had planned. When I asked Him to change my heart so that my prayers would reflect His plans for me, my prayer requests began to change too!

As I began to pray the prayers He had planted in my heart, He answered those prayers—they were what He put there. The best part was that I was able to see God

faithful provisions

Weekly Grocery
Budget List

Store: ....
Total $ ....

Quantity	Item (Coupons)	Total Cost

save money. live generously.

at work in my life in the smallest of ways, but to me, they were huge! I could feel my Creator walking with me, side by side in this journey, knowing He had my back, knowing He would never leave me or forsake me. I finally knew, deep in my heart, that I was indeed more valuable to Him than the birds He created. He provides completely for them, and He will provide even more so for me.

. . . .

Consider the ravens: They do not sow or reap, they have no storeroom or barn; yet God feeds them. And how much more valuable you are than birds!

LUKE 12:24

. . . .

Planning with Prayer

I firmly believe prayer is one of the best planning tools. Asking the heavenly Father to help you be a good steward of what He has blessed you with is ultimately what He wants for you. As I told you, I have found that what I want is not usually the best plan. But what God wants is always the best plan. Let me share an analogy to give you a visual on how important it is to be in submission to God's plan for us.

There was a little boy who went to the store with his father. His father told him he could pick out any toy in the store, but it could only be one. He could have whatever toy he chose. "But," he told the boy, "the best toy is the one I will pick for you, and it is in the back of the store, so trust me!" The father and son walked into the store and immediately the boy was distracted by all the toy train displays and remote control cars in the front of the store. He kept grabbing things, and his father gently reminded him that the best gift was yet to come. The boy obediently listened, trusting that his father was right. As they got to the back of the store, there was a wall full of bicycles. The father led his son over to the most beautiful, shiny red bike in the entire store. The boy was beyond words; he was just beaming! He looked at his father and smiled and said, "Daddy, how did you know?" The father replied, "Son, I know you better than anyone and I was once a boy myself. I know exactly what you want before you do!"

This is just like it is with God the Father. He sent His Son to walk in our shoes. He knows exactly what we are feeling and what we need. If we trust in Him, He will lead us to all the blessings He has in store for us. Our job is just to trust Him.

· ·

If you believe, you will receive whatever you ask for in prayer.

MATTHEW 21:22

· ·

So remember to pray before planning, and be specific in your prayers! Here is a list of some of my favorite prayer requests to help you in this new journey. Ask the Lord for:

- ◊ Enjoyment in the process
- ◊ Meals to please and bless your family
- ◊ Time to thoughtfully prepare each week
- ◊ God's hand in decision-making
- ◊ Eyes to "see" the deals
- ◊ Self-control in budgeting

One of my favorite stories is one a reader shared with me. While she was at checkout one day, and on a very tight budget, she knew she had more than she could pay for in her cart. As she was walking up to the checkout, she said a quick prayer that God would reveal to her what she needed to remove. It turns out that the item she removed ended up being something she didn't realize she already had at home! These are the kinds of interactions that really show me God is with me in every detail of my life.

Nothing is ever too small to pray for.

Chapter 7

. . . .

THE GROCERY TRIP

Now that you have your planning done, it is time to go to the store. There are a few more things you should know and a few more things you should do before heading out. Again, these will not only help you save money but time.

Establish a Shopping Day

Part of your plan should include an established shopping day. The day may change depending on what life serves up for you during any given week, but take a look at the week ahead and plan what day you will shop. Many stores have an appointed day for senior citizens to shop at a discount, for example, so make those opportunities part of your consideration if you qualify.

This is good for a couple of reasons. First, it establishes a habit or routine for you. Second, if you are going to visit more than one store in a week, it will help you plan your trips. For instance, a certain store I like to shop is twenty miles away, so it is not convenient to go there except occasionally. If they have a really good deal on something, I will plan to stop there on a Thursday. Why Thursday? That's the day I travel down a major interstate from my suburban home to the heart of Nashville every week for a standing appointment. On my return trip, I just exit the interstate, run into the store with my already-planned-out list in hand, and grab my items. I can do that in less time than it would take me to get there in one leg of the trip! Remember, I only make this extra stop when there is a good deal and I'm in the area.

Retailers know that the longer you can keep a customer in a store, the more they will spend. So, my goal is to shop as little as possible each week. This can change depending on the week, but my overall goal is to pick one day of the week in which to get most of my shopping done. Depending on my schedule and where I want to go, it could mean it is split up between a few days. If I happen to be in the kitchen and I find I am missing an ingredient, I do my best to use a substitute or go without, because my goal is to minimize my time at the store and time running around to stores.

How Many Stores to Shop?

Many people think I chase every deal that I post on my blog, FaithfulProvisions.com. Well, here's a heads-up: I don't. In fact, since my second child was born, I feel like I am doing good to get to even *one* store each week!

Earlier, I suggested that you shop at only one store when you start this savvy saving lifestyle. Then, as you become more advanced and your season of life allows, you can shop for good deals at multiple stores. Here are the benefits of each method.

Shop at Only One Store

When you begin, don't feel like you have to chase down every deal in town. I strongly suggest shopping at one store until you get comfortable. For many of you, that will be the store you already visit most often. Stick with it. Why? Familiarity.

- ◇ You spend less time hunting for items because you know where everything is.
- ◇ You quickly learn store-specific sales cycles.
- ◇ You learn the store brand, and you know which store brand foods are the ones your family enjoys.
- ◇ You will get to know the managers, department heads, and employees—and when they mark things down.

Rest assured, stocking ahead and saving tons of money is going to work for you even if there is only one store in your shopping rotation.

Shopping at Multiple Stores

When you are comfortable with this way of grocery purchasing and you are ready to stock up, going to multiple stores is a great way to jump-start your stockpile. In my situation, I live near several grocery stores that are a few minutes' drive from home. Once this way of shopping becomes your habit, you can pick and choose where and how often you shop.

As for me, I shop mostly at one store because I have two young children. So to accommodate their naptimes and schedules, I limit my shopping to one store. When my kids get a little older and my time begins to free up some, I will go back to adding more stores to my rotation so that I can take advantage of more deals and thus have more goods to donate.

> *My grocery store list consists of two categories: what we "need" for the week and items that we would "want." I have an amount that I would like to try to spend for groceries. If I am under that amount, I will buy items from the "want" category. This was especially helpful when my children were smaller and went grocery shopping with me! They did not ask for items as we went through the store. They knew if they helped me find the best deals and we were under budget, they got to pick out something special!*
>
> *—Bonnie*

> *I meal plan with a detailed grocery list, so that when I go shopping, I am less likely to spend extra. And we are on a cash-only budget, so if it isn't there, it isn't spent!*
>
> *—Chrissy*

Where You Should Shop and Why

One of the most common questions I get asked on FaithfulProvisions.com and at our workshops are, "What are the best stores to shop?" and "What are the best things to get at each type of store?"

There are four main types of stores, and each has a different focus and business model. Knowing that they are different and how their store policies work can really help you navigate toward some amazing savings.

Grocery Stores

The most frequented places where many purchase their groceries include Kroger (and its family of stores), Albertson's, Tom Thumb, Safeway, Dominick's, Publix, Hyvee, and even Whole Foods. A grocery store is a place where the predominant items carried are food. You will see toiletries, cleaning supplies, and more, but the majority of the store space is used to display food items.

Pros. Most of the sales and specials at these stores are around food items, so you can typically get the best deals on food products. They also tend to cater to couponers, having store policies like doubling coupons which draw in more savvy grocery shoppers. Grocery stores are your best bet for stocking up on food products.

Cons. Since the principal items you find in these stores are groceries, you might need to shop around to get all your home shopping done—optical, automotive, etc.—and to get deep discounts on items like toiletries, cleaning supplies, and paper products.

Big-Box Stores

With stores like Walmart and Target offering groceries, you are seeing a move toward purchasing groceries and all other home items in one place. These are stores where you can get almost anything you need in one location. Despite the fact that they tout lower prices, you typically won't see as deep a discount as you will at a traditional grocery store. Big-box stores have more products at smaller discounts, versus a grocery store where you will find deep discounts on some items. Big-box stores aren't usually ideal for shoppers who like to stock up on deeply discounted items.

Pros. You can get all your shopping completed in one place—grocery, automotive, optical, pharmacy, photo, and more. It is more convenient.

Cons. Most big box stores don't have the best coupon policies, such as doubling coupons. You typically only find this policy at grocery stores.

Drugstores

With couponing on the rise, drugstores have given grocery stores a run for their money when it comes to medicine, toiletries, and cleaning items. Of late, I can even get better deals on packaged items like cereal and peanut butter.

Pros. Amazing coupon policies and rewards programs can be found at drugstores. By utilizing rewards programs, you can get the deepest discounts on toiletries, medicine, and cleaning products.

Cons. In order to continue deep savings at a drugstore, you have to routinely shop at the store to capture the best savings using their rewards programs. You can't typically drop in once to get a good deal. You have to "chase the deals," which can get tiresome. The best deals can be had by shopping weekly and using the rewards to purchase new sale items. Also, drugstores do not double coupons like grocery stores do. Sometimes you pay more out of pocket, but get it back in the form of "rewards" that are not necessarily true savings. You are exchanging your cash for that store's reward currency.

Warehouse Clubs

Over the past five years, warehouse clubs like Costco, BJ's and Sam's Club have increased their product categories for the average home purchaser for bulk buying. This makes them more appealing for many. For instance, most warehouse clubs offer a variety of products such as produce, dairy, and even home items and clothing at very deep discounts. You will find the best discounts on most food items in a warehouse club. However, be forewarned, just because it is a wholesale store doesn't mean you are getting wholesale prices. When purchasing in bulk, you must calculate prices per unit. I tend to find toiletries, cleaning supplies, and paper products have a higher per unit cost in warehouse stores than many grocery stores. I typically find the best prices on prepackaged snacks, organic varieties, and even produce. The best strategy for a wholesale club is to purchase items that typically don't go on sale or that you don't have coupons for. For me, this translates to higher-priced items like gourmet coffee and cheeses, produce, organic products, and nuts or dried fruits.

The best strategy for a wholesale club is to purchase items that typically don't go on sale or that you don't have coupons for.

Pros. If you watch per unit prices, you can really save at warehouse clubs. I typically purchase coffee at a wholesale club because I can't find it on sale anywhere near the everyday wholesale price!

Cons. The biggest drawback to warehouse clubs is the annual membership fee. We purchase gas at our wholesale store, which makes it worth the cost of the yearly fee. Or we ask for a membership as a present for Christmas or a birthday. You also need to be very careful with per unit prices, because even if it is a deal, sometimes the bulk purchase is too much for your family at one time, especially on perishable foods. Lastly, warehouse clubs don't take coupons unless they are their own coupon booklets, and usually these prices are raised before the booklet comes out, so there aren't real savings. Plus, you tend to make more impulse buys, which are much pricier than traditional grocery stores. However, many wholesale clubs do accept formula checks that the baby formula companies send new mothers.

Stock Your Shopping Tote

The Boy Scouts motto is "Be prepared." AAA Auto Club says to always have emergency supplies like jumper cables and a flashlight in your car. In this same spirit, I suggest you have a designated shopping tote that you keep in the car at all times stocked with helpful items. Having these items will make your shopping trip go more smoothly and is just one more way to stay organized. I keep my shopping tote in my car with that week's shopping list and sale ads so that when I am near the store I can pop in and not have to worry about planning. I just go when it is most convenient for me. If I have them all in one place, I never have to run around looking for my list, coupons, or sale ads.

Here are some of my suggestions to stock your shopping tote with:

- *Store ads.* Keep a current store ad in your tote so you have the information at your fingertips or grab one as you walk into the store.

- *Coupon file.* Remember, keeping your coupons organized is key, but having them with you is what seals the deal. Don't forget that one of the most important savings strategies you have is being organized.

- *Calculator.* Be sure to keep a calculator of some sort on hand, either one on your phone or bring a small manual version.

- *Pen and paper.* As a society, we are trending toward electronic everything, but keep a pen (or pencil) and paper handy to jot down notes so you can remember to get things like rain checks at checkout when a store is out of an item.

- *Small notepad.* I keep a 3x5 spiral notebook on hand to keep track of my spending at each store, or to take notes on things I might want to look for when I get home.

There are lots of smartphone apps to help you in your grocery shopping, such as The Better Buy and Cellfire. See chapter 8 for a list of helpful smartphone apps.

- *Paper clips.* Keep a few extra paper clips on hand to help sort and organize your coupons. This keeps them in one place and not on the grocery store floor or in the parking lot!

- *Scissors.* I keep a small set on hand to clip a coupon while in the store. Many times I will find a booklet or store flyer I hadn't previously seen and cutting coupons with scissors looks much better than ripping it out, possibly ruining the bar code.

- *Snacks*—Keeping a few snacks in your tote is great for you and your kids while shopping. If your children are young and have to go with you to the store, food can be a great distraction and help you to stay on the task at hand: saving money. Also, you won't be as prone to make impulse buys if you are full.

Navigating the Store

Have you noticed that every store you shop in is different? Even stores in the same chain vary layouts and policies per location. One of the first things you need to do as an informed shopper is to understand all the policies, find out about store programs, and even get to know the employees at *your* store. All these things will help in making it a better shopping experience.

Know Your Store's Policies

As we saw in chapter 6, store policies vary depending on the type of store, where it is located, and even the type of clientele it pulls in. As a savvy shopper, there are questions you can ask at your store so you can be fully prepared to save money. In addition to the checklist of questions provided in chapter 6, here are some other questions to get you familiar with your store. This is also a great opportunity to get to know the store employees and learn about programs you might never have been aware of otherwise.

- ◇ Do you have a clearance section of marked-down items?

- ◇ What days or time of day do you mark down meat, dairy, and produce for items that are expiring? (At some stores you can go to the store that afternoon to pick up great manager markdowns!)

- ◇ Does your butcher slice whole meat into steaks as a courtesy? Does your deli slice deli meat and cheese blocks as a free service?

- ◇ Do you offer store credit for using reusable bags? (Some stores offer three to five cents per bag credit to bring back your reusable cloth bags.)

Get to Know Employees

One of the best ways to find in-store deals and markdowns is to interact with the department personnel and managers. In my stores, I have found out how they determine department markdowns and what time of day those take effect. This helps me determine when or if I will shop at a particular store each week. For instance, if I know I want marked-down bread from the bakery, I usually plan my trip around a certain time of day. I know when the markdowns are done each day in that department.

SAVING SAVVY TIP

If you have young children, pack a couple of toys and a snack in your shopping tote to keep them occupied while you shop.

As the staff gets to know and recognize you, other benefits will follow. For example, in my local store, Amy marks down the bread every afternoon at a certain time. One day I came in and she hadn't started yet, so I moved on and planned on hitting that department as we were finishing up our trip. When she saw me, she told me to look through items with a certain date and she would go ahead and mark them down for me! This was a nice time savings for me, because knowing myself; I probably would have forgotten to swing back by after my other shopping.

Shop at One Store

To start off, you need to just shop at one store. As you migrate to a more advanced level, you can easily add on more stores, but master the art of *your* store first. Shop where you feel most comfortable and can navigate the easiest. I know that if I go to a new store where I don't understand their store policies and can't find things, I don't save as much as I do in a store where I know the layout and store policies.

If I shop at one store it also helps me get in and out more quickly. I know where everything is. As I mentioned in chapter 6, a big time saver is to write your grocery list in order of the store layout. It prevents backtracking and cuts down on your time in the store. You save money and reduce impulse buys by merely cutting back the time you are in the store.

Shop the Perimeter

The perimeters of most stores are laid out with produce, meat, and dairy. The processed, prepackaged, and more expensive items tend to be shelved in the center of the store. As your savvy shopping journey is beginning, if you do nothing else, your best tip is to shop the perimeter of the store, instantly keeping your spending down.

Now that you know how to navigate your store, you need to pick up the store sale ad next.

Bring Your Store Ads

As we have seen, grocery store sale ads can have lots of great information in them. Among the most important are the details of what items the store has on sale. If I know the size and variety of the item that is on sale on my list, it makes it easier for me when going through the store. Sometimes I go to the store the day before the ads change over, which means the clerks are getting ready for the new sales, so some of the sale labels have been removed. This can be very confusing! If I have my sale ad with me and a detailed grocery list, I know what I need without second guessing. It also alerts me at checkout if I have picked up the wrong item, because it won't ring up on sale.

Stick to Your Shopping List to Prevent Impulse Buys

Having a detailed grocery list will help you stop impulse buys. When I used to shop without a list I would look at things (usually on the end caps) and think, *Maybe we need that!* Of course, those end caps are designed to be moneymakers for the store and the manufacturer. They are strategically placed to grab your attention. Sometimes they are good deals, but often they are not. Flashy "low price" signs do not always mean you are getting a good price. When I get distracted and veer off my list, it can be those few items on the end caps that make up a large chunk of my spending. That's why I have to stick to my list! I know what I need, and it is on that sheet of paper!

> " *At the store, I have found that if I stay true to my list, I spend less because I am not buying things I do not need!* "
>
> —Jessica

Using Rain Checks

A rain check is a store coupon to purchase a sale ad item that is out of stock. For example, say your grocery is selling milk at the rock-bottom price of $1 per gallon. When you get to the store, they are all out of skim. You can go to the customer service desk and ask for a rain check to use the next time you are in the store. That means that the next time you shop, no matter what the price of milk, you may use your rain check to get it at the sale price of $1 per gallon. Many stores will even substitute a similar item in lieu of a rain check. Just don't forget to remind your cashier at checkout!

Rain checks might sound like an old way of doing things, but they're a great way to save. Here are some things to keep in mind when using them:

Expiration dates. I have found that most stores do not put an expiration date on the rain check. That really comes in handy for me when I am over budget and would like to get the item. I can wait until I am more within my budget to use the rain check.

Limits. See if the item for which you are requesting a rain check has a limit on the number you can purchase. Many stores will limit the amount of that purchase on really good deals.

Handing over rain checks. When I am checking out, I try to hold out my items that have rain checks until the very end. Then I hand over the rain check right before the checker scans the item. If he scans the item before he knows I have a rain check for it, he will have to "price override" the item. By giving him the rain check first, this just saves him the hassle.

Rain checks for items matched with expiring coupons. A few times I have had a coupon set to expire the day I am at the store and if the store is out of the item, I am out of luck. Many stores will honor a coupon even if it is expired when they don't have the product stocked at that time. I have found that they will typically just staple the expired coupons to the rain check and let you come back the next week. It always pays to ask.

Check Your Grocery Total

Most people think you only need to tally up your spending if you are on a tight budget. Well, there are plenty of other benefits. Let's face it, things can get pretty hectic in the checkout lane. It is hard to watch every item scan, especially if you are trying to watch a child or two at the same time! So don't forget to go through your budgeted weekly grocery list and do the math at home. And put that total plus tax at the top of your list. This way, you know what total to expect at checkout. Plus, if you get overcharged for an item, you can quickly figure it out, and many stores will give you the item free.

A few weeks ago, I was in the checkout lane purchasing our favorite cut of meat, rib eye. It was marked down to $4.88/pound for the whole rib eye roast. I had asked the butcher to cut me four rib eye steaks out of it, because I didn't need the whole thing. When he rang it up per pound, he rang it up as the whole rib eye roast, not just the portion I had gotten. So my checkout total was $70 over what I had circled at the top of my list to spend! Guess what? I really wish I had gotten more steaks that day, because he gave the steaks to me free because the price rang up wrong. That's great motivation to watch those totals.

SAVING SAVVY TIP

If you get overcharged for an item at checkout, many stores will give you the item that rings up wrong for free.

Do you feel prepared to make that grocery trip armed with all your newfound knowledge? As I said in the beginning, there is a wealth of information I have provided for you here, but remember you don't need to do it all. Simply begin by picking a few things you can easily and quickly implement to start seeing some savings in your own personal budget. Choose the tools that fit into your lifestyle, season of life, and time allotment.

I know you will do wonderfully. The key is to use what you've learned in this chapter and start applying your very own customized money-saving strategies!

SAVINGS STRATEGIES FOR
THE GROCERY TRIP

IF YOU HAVE *MORE* TIME . . .

1. **Shop multiple stores.** If you are able, shopping the sales at multiple stores will save you more money.

2. **Fill a shopping tote.** Get a shopping tote and fill it with all the things you will need for each shopping trip.

3. **Know your store.** Before you shop, call your store and look online for their policies and loyalty programs.

4. **Use a shopping list template.** Create your own template or use the downloadable Grocery Shopping List template on FaithfulProvisions.com before you hit the store.

. . . .

IF YOU HAVE **LESS** TIME . . .

1. **Set a shopping day.** Establish a shopping day as part of your routine.

2. **Shop one store.** If you are low on time, you can save greatly by just sticking with one store. It takes a little longer, but can easily be done.

3. **Read store ads.** While you are shopping, make sure you have a store ad in hand at all times to verify product, sizes, varieties, and price.

4. **Use rain checks.** If your store is out of an item, grab a rain check so you can get it next time.

5. **Check your receipt.** Before you walk out of the store, check your receipt to make sure the total is correct. If not, you can fix it at customer service, preventing extra trips.

Chapter 8

MORE SAVINGS STRATEGIES

When you plan meals, stock up, and use coupons, you come to expect more for your money and effort. With that in mind, I have a few more savings strategies you can use to help boost your shopping savings.

Take Advantage of Rebates

A great way to save is to take advantage of rebate programs. A rebate is money you get back after purchasing an item. The best way to use a rebate program is in conjunction with a sale and a coupon. For instance, let's say that Kellogg's cereal goes on sale for $1.99 a box, and there is a $1 off one box coupon available. Plus, if you purchase four boxes you get $4 back in a rebate. You would end up getting all four boxes for free! Here is how it looks:

> **Kellogg's Cereal—on sale $1.99 per box**
> Use [4] $1/1 Kellogg's Cereal Coupons
> Submit for $4 when you buy 4 boxes of Kellogg's Cereal Rebate
> **Final Price: 4 boxes for FREE**

There are many different types of rebate programs you can take advantage of. The difference in these is in the timing and information needed to process the rebate.

Mail-In Rebates

A mail-in rebate is where you purchase an item and fill out a form, including UPC symbols and a receipt, to send in to the company offering it. Usually within six to eight weeks you will receive the rebate in the mail in the form of a check. I don't recommend doing this unless it is a decent value rebate. If it is only a dollar or two, I usually pass, because the time involved and the postage to send it turn the rebate into nothing but time wasted.

All-in-One Rebates

This rebate is where you send in a rebate form to be reimbursed for multiple products at one time. For instance, a retailer might have one hundred items that all have $1 and $2 rebates. However, with these kinds of rebates you typically do not have to send in a UPC symbol. Many allow you to enter the receipt information into an online form. If you have a lot of items that match up with coupons, this can be a very good option.

Instant Rebates

An instant rebate is usually given back at the time of checkout, in the form of a coupon to use at the store on your next visit. Some stores use catalina coupons or store receipts to redeem the savings. I typically find these to be part of a store savings event. For instance, Kroger and its family of stores frequently has a Mega-Item Event, where you get a dollar amount back at checkout for purchasing participating items. Here is an example:

> *Buy 4 Biscuit Rolls and get $2 off at Checkout*
> **Biscuit Rolls—$1.66**
> Use [4] $1/1 Biscuit Rolls coupons
> Out of Pocket: $2.64
> Receive $2 store credit at checkout
> **Final Price: $.16/ea when you buy 4 Biscuit Rolls**

Store Rewards Programs

With a store reward program, you purchase participating products that earn you "rewards." Many times the reward is worth the entire price of the item. This program is different from a mail-in rebate because instead of getting a check that you cash and use anywhere, you get a "reward" in the form of a store credit. The main advantage of store rewards is that these are usually substantial savings and will get you products free without ever using a coupon. Pair coupons with these items to turn them into "money-maker" deals. I typically see these types of programs at drugstores, office supply stores, and retail locations.

Cash-Back Sites

If you like to shop online, I highly recommend checking out cash-back sites like Ebates.com or ShopatHome.com. You earn a percentage of your total purchase just for using their portal to purchase your products. Here is how it works: You go to one of the cash-back portals and type in the store name you want to purchase from, say Kohl's. When you click through from the cash-back site, they track your purchases and depending on what deal they have going with the merchant you can earn anywhere from 3 to 15 percent back on your purchases. These typically pay out every month or on a quarterly basis.

Price Matching

Can't find the coupon you need for your favorite grocery store? Try using another supermarket's deals where you normally shop. One way to save money at grocery stores is to play the game they know best: leveraging the competition. It's a win-win situation for everyone, especially you, the consumer.

Two major national retailers now offer price matching (sometimes called "ad matching") to their consumers. Currently, both Walmart and Target allow you to take an ad from a competitor and bring it in to get the best price on your everyday purchases. Typically they only match grocery stores' advertised prices for individual items, and they don't include BOGOF sales or coupons in grocery store ads. Always ask about your store's price matching policy before shopping.

As I have mentioned, be sure to ask your store if they accept competitors' coupons. Each store, even chain stores, have different competitors, depending on what other stores are nearby. Check your grocery store's website, as well as other local stores' sites, to look for store coupons. Many retailers allow you to use a competitor's coupon just to keep you in their store. Stores don't want to lose your business. These days, they know how price-conscious consumers are.

Ditch Brand Loyalty

In order to save the most when using coupons, you need to be flexible with your brand choices. Since the best savings strategy is to use coupons combined with a sale, the brands available will vary with each sales cycle. While I am brand loyal on a few items, which is perfectly fine, I have learned that it's better to yield my preferences to what's on sale for the bulk of my purchases. If you are brand loyal on a few items, just be sure to stock up on those items when you find them on sale. Variety is the spice of life—and the key to saving more money!

Create Your Own Price List

In chapter 2 we talked about the advantages of using a price list, like the one available as a free download on FaithfulProvisions.com. But if you want to really save big, you can create your own customized price list that fits the stores you shop at with the specific items you purchase by brand. This particularly comes in handy if you have a family that has dietary restrictions such as allergies or diabetes, or if you are trying to eat organic.

Get a spiral notebook. Buy a small spiral notebook and keep it in your grocery tote. Use this to jot down prices as you see things on sale. You can keep a catalog of what was on sale, at what price, and which store.

Organize your list by food category. Have a page for each category of food you want to track prices on. For example, have a page for meats, produce, and more.

Log the prices and store. Write down the price of the item when it is on sale and where you found it. You might find trends, like only one store ever has particular items on sale; then you can know that anytime you stock up on that particular item, for the best price you will only purchase it from that store.

Faithful Provisions
Price List Download

Once you get started on these steps, you will eventually have your own customized price list that reflects the lowest price for which you can purchase each item on your weekly lists. And don't forget to download the free Provisions iPhone app or Price List from Faithful Provisions to help you create your own customized price list.

Make Your Own Snack Bags

Unless it is at a great discount after coupons and a sale, I don't buy convenience foods like prepackaged, snack-size crackers or carrot sticks. Again, I purchase in bulk or in a larger quantity, and then I dole them out into zippered snack bags. Packing my own snack-size options not only cuts down on my spending, but it provides me the opportunity to have healthy snacks on hand that are ready to eat.

Food Redesigns: Cook Once, Eat Twice

In chapter 4, you saw the benefits of weekly meal planning. If you're ready to save even more money, you can take meal plans one step further by cooking once and eating twice (or even three times!). This is one of my very favorite ways to cook. Simply put, when I cook something like pot roast or chicken, I cook enough so that I can use the meat in two or three additional meals. Instead of cooking a two- to three-pound pot roast, I will cook a five- to six-pound one. The first night we will have pot roast and mashed potatoes, but for the next several nights I can easily and quickly make things like French dip sandwiches, beef stroganoff, or even beef enchiladas—all from the first night's leftover pot roast dinner! When I find pot roast on sale for a great deal at the store, I freeze a couple. Then when we are ready for it, I just prepare one and add all the extras to that week's meal plan.

Not only can this be applied to meat, but it works with other staples like pasta or rice. When I cook brown rice, which usually takes thirty to forty-five minutes, I make at least four extra servings. If I don't have any reason for it at that time, I will freeze it in single-serving bags to use later. The same goes for pasta. Another good example of my food redesigns is with this meal: pork loin, carrot salad, and whole grain rice. I will translate those leftovers into pork fried rice later in the week, because I can dice the pork and use the extra carrot and rice to fill out the meal! This is so easy, and it makes for less clean-up—my kind of meal!

Be Creative with Leftovers

You know all the extras you end up throwing away at the end of every meal? What if you could repurpose them or use them for another meal later? One of the biggest time and money savers I learned was to be creative with the food that was left after dinner was finished. Whether it was extra chopped veggies that weren't needed for the pizza or the last bits of ham, I find a way to use them again in another meal. I might save those extra veggies for a soup next week, or use the ham bits or hock in a bean soup. My biggest trick is to just freeze it, label it, and then put it on my Freezer Inventory List.

I like to make homemade bread, so when I have put the time into making it, I want to use every bit of it. If we have ends that never get eaten, I might drop them in the food processor and freeze as bread crumbs, or cut into quarters and bake in the oven for homemade croutons.

Here are a few of my favorite tips to make the ingredients go further.

- ◇ *Freeze meat and vegetable scraps.* When I purchase or make a rotisserie chicken or have leftover Thanksgiving turkey, I freeze the carcass to make homemade stock later when I have the time. I also keep a plastic bowl in the freezer for vegetable scraps like onion or carrot peel, and celery hearts to throw into the stock. This way I am not using the prime cut of the vegetables; I just need the flavor, which is usually best coming from its unused portions.

- ◇ *Save liquids in ice cube trays.* If I have leftover sauces from a pasta or pizza, or juice from drained or leftover canned fruits, or even uneaten smoothies, I put them into ice cube trays to use for later. I can either thaw the sauce for individual use or drop the frozen juice into a smoothie.

Batch Cooking

Buying in bulk doesn't always mean you save, so it depends on what you are buying and why. I frequently purchase meat in bulk when it is on sale. But that also means I have to do something with it immediately. I like to double up on recipes and freeze the extras for later. If I have the time, I do "mini kitchen prep days" by preparing a whole batch of, say, grilled chicken. When I find chicken breasts on sale, I'll buy in bulk, say eight to ten pounds or so, and do "batch cooking." This is where you cook all the chicken at one time and then plan out all the meals you will use it in. My favorite way to use chicken is to grill it, then slice it up and freeze it to use later for salads,

LIVING Generously TIP

If you do batch cooking, double the portions for at least one meal before you freeze it. That way, you can invite friends or neighbors to share a meal with you—and you'll already have enough food prepared!

soups, sandwiches, or quesadillas. Instead of purchasing the precooked and sliced chicken breasts in the deli section, I have created my own for a fraction of the price.

Plan Dinner Out

Yes, we eat out. There is nothing better than a night off from cooking, planning, and cleaning. Don't you agree? But, it is not quite worth it if it costs my entire week's grocery budget to do it. We try to plan one meal out per week. Lately it has been our Sunday lunch. But in doing so, we are very purposeful and strategic about it. We don't just decide where we want to go and head out. Just like the other food planning, we grab our restaurant and retail coupon books, Groupons, and any other deals we have on restaurants and decide from there. Because we have two young children, our first choice is usually a place that has a generous kids' menu, or kids-eat-free days.

A few weeks ago we had a gift card to a popular local restaurant. I was ready to go the day we got the card, but by signing up for the restaurant's e-mail newsletter, I was informed of some upcoming "kids eat free" nights. So we planned our dinner out around that. To make the deal even sweeter, I got a free dessert coupon in my inbox the week we were going. We had a great dinner out for four for under twenty dollars. That is a deal. But do you see the difference? Our dinner out was purposeful and planned; it wasn't impulsive. This is what makes a night out so worth it. Gift cards to our favorite restaurants are one of the top things on our gift ideas for family members. They are easy, and our family knows we can make a gift card go really far!

Use Smartphone Apps

With all the amazing technology available I didn't want to pass over pointing out free smartphone resources that will help you in your cooking, grocery planning, and shopping. Here are a few that have come recommended to aid you in saving.

A few popular grocery list apps that allow you to share lists with family members are:

- Grocery IQ
- Our Groceries
- Shop Simple
- Ziplist

The Better Buy

Take the prices for two comparable items, enter the price and the quantity (e.g., 24 cans, 12 rolls, 14.5 oz, etc.) for items and The Better Buy will tell you which is the better deal.

Cellfire

You can check for manufacturer's coupons on your phone while shopping, select the ones you want, and usually within fifteen to twenty minutes they are loaded onto your store loyalty card for checkout.

Coupon Sherpa

Uses geo-location or zip code to suggest the closest locations to use retailer coupons.

Kroger

Add e-coupons to your store loyalty card while in the store shopping.

Price Grabber

A price comparison search engine that searches both online and bricks-and-mortar stores for the best prices.

Sale Saver

Designed to calculate your final total after all discounts, simply enter in the original or sale price on the tag, then enter the clearance discount and any coupons or additional markdowns you have. Within seconds you have your deal price.

Yowza

This geographic locator app helps you find coupons for merchants from one to fifty miles of your location.

Follow Faithful Provisions.com

Here is one final savings tip you can use and it won't cost you a dime. You can follow my website, FaithfulProvisions.com, in a variety of ways. Just pick the one that works best for you.

- ◇ subscribe to free e-mail updates at FaithfulProvisions.com
- ◇ "like" Faithful Provisions on Facebook: http://www.facebook.com/faithfulprovisions
- ◇ follow Faithful Provisions on Twitter: http://twitter.com/faithfulprov
- ◇ subscribe to my RSS Feed: www.faithfulprovisions.com/feed
- ◇ subscribe to my feed via a feed reader: www.google.com/reader

Faithful Provisions
Subscribe Page

Chapter 9

A LIFESTYLE OF GENEROSITY

Winston Churchill once said, "You make a living by what you get. You make a life by what you give." Churchill was a great leader, and what he said about giving really drives home the point of what I think generosity can be: a lifestyle.

Lifestyles are defined as typical ways of living and there are probably as many different lifestyles as there are people. I'm not advocating a vow of poverty or putting your family at risk. I'm not for having so much stuff on hand that your home looks like a department store or a hoarder. What I am talking about is thinking of others "as you go." When you are at the store and find products you can get for free, but wouldn't use yourself, could you get them to donate?

. . . .

Feed the hungry, and help those in trouble. Then
your light will shine out from the darkness, and the
darkness around you will be as bright as noon.

ISAIAH 58:10 NLT

. . . .

When I teach my Faithful Provisions workshops, I often share about an experience I had and how it impacted a young, homeless mother in recovery at the Nashville Rescue Mission. The rescue mission is a place where men and women come in from the cold, get clean, and learn new life skills. I was going to teach a coupon class for the women and brought some extra toiletries to donate. One of the items was something I didn't need and had considered not buying in the first place. Even after I brought it home, I considered throwing it away, but the thought occurred to me that maybe someone could use it, so I put it in the box with the other items. When the workshop was over, all the women picked items from the box. One woman picked up the item I almost didn't buy. This young mother was so thankful to have it, she came up to me after the workshop to tell me how great it was to have it. I realized then, that even the smallest of things can make a big difference in someone else's life.

What Is Living Generously?

To me, living generously is:

- ◇ using your God-given ability to help those in need
- ◇ where your time, money, and talents come together to meet the needs of others
- ◇ something you can practice all year long, not just at Christmastime

If you have received salvation from Christ, you have been given the gift of eternal life from God. So, in a very fundamental way, you have already been shown great generosity. The least we can all do is use these gifts to help others in need. Some have more material resources to pull from, some have time, and some just have a big heart. Others have unique talents that can benefit people. No matter what the gift, being generous with your gifts is the key.

So let's look at three main components of living generously: time, money, and talents.

. . . .

You will be enriched in every way so that you
can be generous on every occasion, and . . . your
generosity will result in thanksgiving to God.

2 CORINTHIANS 9:11

. . . .

Generous with Your Time

Time is something we all have and spend. Many of us, me included, have spent it well at times, and have wasted it at other times. But, since we all have the same twenty-four hours in a day, why not begin to use some of it in a noble, fruitful way to benefit others? Not because we have to, but because we want to. It has been said many times and many ways that time is an asset. Being generous with your time can be as simple as a phone call or e-mail of encouragement to someone who needs it. That simple act costs you very little but can make a big impact on the other person.

One way you can use your time generously is by picking up extra items at the grocery each week as you do your regular shopping trip. If you are already clipping coupons and searching for the best deals, take five more minutes to clip extra coupons for items you may not need or want but would be great donation items. For instance, we have pasta coming out our ears. But this week it is on sale again, and my coupons make it less than ten cents a box. If I would just take a little extra time when I am doing my grocery planning, I can grab anywhere from five to ten boxes of pasta for under a dollar to donate. Think of how much you could help others if you do this every week.

" *I use the money from one of my part-time jobs to buy healthy snack foods
for the homeless teenagers that attend our high school. Living out of their
cars or sleeping on friends' couches, they are on their own for food outside*

169

of school hours. I like to think my snack packs full of peanut butter, raisins, cheese crackers, granola bars, etc., help them get through the nights and weekends a little easier. I always include a little note of encouragement with a Scripture verse to feed their souls too! "

—*Julie*

Now that is an example of not wasting time. Working more than one job and helping to provide healthy snacks for homeless teens is generous. I think my favorite part of Julie's story is the "little note of encouragement with a Scripture verse to feed their souls."

I know of another couple who babysat for free on a Friday night as a gift to several families during the Christmas season. We all know how busy that time of year is and how hard it can be to find a sitter. This was a great gift because it brought together about thirty kids in a safe environment to watch cartoons, face-paint, draw pictures, eat cookies, and watch child-appropriate movies while the parents got some shopping done. What a great picture of living generously!

Being generous with time can be helping a neighbor with yard work or sweeping the snow off their steps. It can be providing a meal to a single-parent family or volunteering with a local charity. I know one lady who used to take her magazine subscriptions to a local nursing home, along with all of her free toiletries. She would package them up in gift baskets and visit the residents' rooms. Needless to say, she was the bright spot in their day!

· ·

Each of you should give what you have decided
in your heart to give, not reluctantly or under
compulsion, for God loves a cheerful giver.
—2 CORINTHIANS 9:7

· ·

Generous with Your Money

Generosity can come in many forms, but I think the first place we recognize generosity is in the form of cash. Most people think of generosity in terms of money, and that certainly is an expression of generosity. So turn that into your form of generosity easily by turning your savings into donations.

Earlier I talked about a paradigm shift in the way you shop. What about a paradigm shift in the way you think about giving? If you are saving money in the checkout line, you can form a plan to set aside some of that money to give away each month. You could use that money in any number of ways. Here are just a few examples of how this could look:

- Sponsor a family by filling their pantry with your extras.
- Contribute food to a local church or food bank.
- Help support overseas ministries.
- Give Angel Tree gifts at Christmas.
- Fill an Operation Christmas Child box.
- Participate in Toys for Tots.
- Provide for men and women at area shelters.
- Contribute to friends who are adopting orphans.
- Sponsor people on mission trips.
- Buy postage to send expired coupons to military families overseas.

Some of the items above we live out and many are ideas I have gotten from readers. Specifically, end-of-season sales bring great prices on everything from clothing to toys. Use these sales as opportunities to stock up on gifts for Angel Tree, Operation Christmas Child boxes, and Toys for Tots events. If you play the drugstore games, which frequently garner you free or inexpensive toiletries and cleaning items, use them to fill gift baskets for nursing homes, shelters, orphanages, or missionaries.

Generous with Your Talents

What have you been gifted with? What talents do you have? Can you play an instrument or sing? Are you good at accounting? Do you own a business that provides a valuable service? Are you an excellent couponer or a wonderful cook? There are many ways to give of your talents and many who can benefit from them.

Take your talents and give them back to God. I encourage you to ask Him what He'd have you do with what He gave you. How could you use your God-given gifts to give back to others? I don't believe God gives us talents for ourselves. I believe he gives them to us so we can serve others and show them the love of Christ. After all, that is our job here on earth, right? It's all about keeping it in perspective.

· ·

It is more blessed to give than to receive.

ACTS 20:35

· ·

Giving and Receiving

The Bible tells us it is more blessed to give than to receive (Acts 20:35). I often wondered exactly what that meant. So we will be more blessed to give, than when we are receiving? How can that be when we are giving of ourselves, whether financially, time, or talents?

I wanted to help someone in need. I didn't do it for years because I kept waiting for the perfect opportunity. Then I began to feel this strong urge to just give somewhere; it didn't matter where.

. . . .

Share your food with the hungry.

ISAIAH 58:7

. . . .

The first opportunity that came up for me was an unlikely one. To take a step back, you must know that I have always wanted to go on an overseas mission trip. Since having children, this has become a less desirable dream because I have some big responsibilities here and I need to prioritize. Little did I know that God would fulfill that desire in a very unique way.

We were sitting in our small group at church one Sunday night and a man named Henry came to tell us about this group he had been working with. It was a group of Sudanese refugees that were in great need here in our own community. They had struggles and challenges I could hardly fathom. He said that they had trouble even keeping food on the table. At that moment a light went on in my head. I knew that God had given me this talent of saving money to be a better steward of what he had given us. But now I was beginning to see that my talents weren't for me alone, God in His great glory had gifted me with something that could bless others. The really neat thing about it was that I could take all my extras once a month down to their center for the refugees to use. While I was there I was able to form some wonderful relationships with the women there. I stayed involved in that organization for a little over a year and it was the most fulfilling season of my life. I got to know people I would never have had the opportunity to meet and serve. God had brought the mission field to me! I love how God turns a situation into something you would never have imagined. He is the ultimate Creator—and creative He is!

The other side of that coin is to receive well. Have you ever been on the other side of giving? Have you been blessed by someone else's generosity? Sometimes, pride can get in the way of a noble, generous gesture. Let's face it: it can be just plain hard to accept someone's generosity. Last year, when Bradford was downsized, among the benefits lost was a company car. In this day and age, having only one car can present some problems. By God's grace, we got by with one for over a year with few hiccups. We were very fortunate to have a family friend who knew of our situation. Without giving it a second thought, they offered up the use of a spare vehicle. It was a kind offer and we accepted it graciously.

> " *My husband has been laid off for two years now. This has been the hardest year and this is also the first time I have ever received food from a charity pantry. But I have to say I am grateful.* "
>
> —*Laura*

Many people find themselves in positions they never thought they would be in, as the lady above. Having to rely on the kindness of others is an uncomfortable position to be in. Remember, your situation can turn on a dime, but being equipped can make all the difference in your attitude.

It doesn't make sense to give out of your need. However, in God's economy, it doesn't work any other way. Before we can be truly blessed, we have to learn how to bless other people. We have to always realize that somebody somewhere is worse off than we are and we can give something. So take an honest look at your life. Are you being stingy with your time? Are you being stingy with your talents? Are you being stingy with your money?

Always remember . . . you have something to give.

Chapter 10

. . . .

BRINGING IT ALL TOGETHER

We have covered a lot of ground in this book, but think about how far you have come! You've learned about:

SAVING SAVVY TIP

♦ Stocking up

♦ Preparing the freezer

♦ Meal planning

♦ Couponing

♦ Reading sale ads

♦ Grocery shopping

♦ Living generously

Consider everything you have learned as new skills to help your family in the goal to save money. So, step out of your comfort zone; these skills will only help if you put them to good use. But I promise you, if you put them to work for you and your family, you *will* save money. Now's the time to put this all together and begin using your new saving savvy.

Don't immediately cut your grocery budget in half. Wait until you have an appropriate stockpile of staple items to lower your budget.

Do First Things First

Taking what you've learned, here is a quick outline to help you prioritize. Every day I hear from readers who are new to this type of shopping that the most difficult thing is knowing where to start in order to maximize their savings and time. There is so much information to sift through, but as we have shown, each person is different and starts at a different place. So here are some tasks in order of what I consider to be the biggest money and time savers.

- ◇ *Clean and organize your pantry, freezer, and fridge.* Use the downloadable Freezer Inventory List from FaithfulProvisions.com to get started.

- ◇ *Determine how much you spend and set a budget.* Look at your bank statements to determine what you spend, then set that as your beginning budget.

- ◇ *Create a weekly meal plan.* Download the Meal Planning Template on FaithfulProvisions.com to make meal planning easy.

- ◇ *Shop with store ads and sales to save big.* On your next grocery store visit, pick up a store ad and begin getting familiar with the sales cycles and what is contained within these ads.

- ◇ *Stock up on your family's staple items.* Start your stockpile with the items you use the most in your home, such as meats, freezer bags, cereal, cleaning supplies, toiletries, and paper products.

- ◇ *Use coupons strategically.* Maximize your savings by using coupons with sales items or clearance items.

- ◇ *Use store sales and match coupons with sale items to save big.* Each week on FaithfulProvisions.com, I post the best deals to make reading the sale ads easier.

- ◇ *Donate your extras.* Give generously with what you have saved: your money, time, and talents.

What the Future Holds

Over the next six to twelve weeks, as you use that extra money to purchase good deals, your meal planning will pull from your growing stockpile. You will find that your grocery list will have fewer needs and more stock-up items on it. Once your "stock-up" items greatly exceed the "needs" on your grocery list, then you can begin to take the steps needed to lower your grocery budget. You are making great strides, but proceed with caution!

Caution: Avoid This Mistake

A big mistake to avoid when changing your shopping mind-set is cutting your budget in half right off the bat. Some people cut their spending in half *immediately*. That is not going to work and here is why: when you begin making this change, you are starting with virtually no stockpile of staple items. You must purchase the food you need to eat right now, plus start stocking ahead on items that you will use in future meals.

Some people actually see a small rise in their spending the first few weeks because they are stocking up. However, if you will incorporate meal planning and prepare meals from items on sale, you can strategically feed your family *and* stock up on your staple items within your current budget.

LIVING Generously TIP

When you create your shopping list template, be sure to include a list of items that your local food pantry needs. Then, as you make your list each week, you will remember to pick up a few extra items to donate to the food pantry.

> *We have a family of five and were spending about $800–$900 each month on groceries. I knew that this was out of control, but didn't know how to fix it. My husband even told me I should clip coupons and I told him it wouldn't work! Ha! Like you teach, it took me a while to see the spending go down. After six months we were down to $400 a month. However, for*

the past month I have consistently been doing $50 a week. Not only do I now save 80 to 90 percent on my groceries, we have been able to give away so much for donations! I tell people that is why I coupon. God has faithfully provided for our family and now, with coupons, I can bless others. 🙶

—*Jennifer*

What to Stock Up on First

SAVING SAVVY TIP

When you find your budget busters on sale, stock ahead on these items first.

For now, let's assume you are just going to eat from what you find on sale in the store ads each week to keep your spending from increasing. If you do this, it will allow you a small cushion of funds in your already established budget to use for stocking ahead. Use these extra funds to purchase the best deals on your staple items, therefore slowly filling up your pantry. We'll talk about exactly how that looks in a minute.

With that said, the first items you need to stock ahead on are your budget busters. Your budget busters are going to depend upon your family and your season of life. For moms with young children, that is going to mean diapers, wipes, formula, and lots of Cheerios. Moms of teenagers will need items like pizza, cereal, and snacks. What is true of almost every season is to stock ahead on the big budget busters: proteins like beef, fish, and chicken.

Here is a visual to give you an idea of how your budgeting percentages will change over time:

BUDGETING PERCENTAGES NOW

80% NEEDS	20% STOCK UP

Now most of your grocery list will be composed of your "needs" or the items you have to purchase to create meals or simple household products and toiletries. The percentage of your list that will entail your stock-up items will be small, comparatively speaking. It will probably look like 80 percent "needs" and about 20 percent "stock up."

FUTURE BUDGETING PERCENTAGES
(3-6 MONTHS)

20% NEEDS	80% STOCK UP

Then, as you move into the future, the percentage of your grocery list that includes your "needs" will slowly shrink. It will look more like the image above. The list will mostly comprise "stock-up" items that you find at a good deal, and you will pick up the "needs" items like milk and produce only. This will dramatically and gradually shift what your list looks like. The "needs" portion of the list will be more like 20 percent of the items and the "stock-up" portion will be most of the list—something like 80 percent.

Adjust your budget as your needs change. It will be in a constant state of flux the first six months while you are working on whittling down your spending. Don't get locked into your budget. It's okay to give yourself a little grace as things change or as you find great stock-up opportunities. Also remember, your budget is going to be different than mine. Everyone's budget is different, so don't try to compare yourself or your budget with anyone else's; your circumstances are different.

Begin Lowering Your Grocery Spending

Reducing your grocery spending doesn't happen overnight, and you're not going to see savings results for at least a couple of weeks. This is a marathon and not a sprint, so be patient. You may not save a lot initially, but that can be expected because you are now purchasing all the things on your list you always buy, plus you are adding your "stock-up" deals too. Again, the learning curve is big, and for you to stick with it and fully understand it will take a few weeks. After all, you need to allow yourself the resources to feed your family.

An Example of How Lowering the Budget Looks

SAVING SAVVY TIP

In the first few weeks, your learning curve is pretty steep, so keep things simple and easy. Add more time-intensive and complicated strategies later.

If all the talk above seems too vague for you and you're still sitting there scratching your head, let's go through an example of how it looks week by week as you try to lower your grocery budget over the course of a three- to six-month time frame. Most couponers find that by six months they are able to dramatically reduce their spending, usually around 50 percent or more.

We are going to start with the assumption that Family A is living on an $800-a-month grocery budget. Within six months, the scenario below is how it will look as they reduce their grocery spending by 50 percent.

WEEKS 1-4

$200 PER WEEK BUDGET

$175 TO MEET IMMEDIATE NEEDS	$25 TOWARD STOCK-UP ITEMS

Most of the budget goes to your immediate needs.

Weeks 1-4: $200/week budget

In the first few weeks you will be eating primarily from the items that are on sale in the weekly grocery store ads, using the few staples you have on hand. All the meals you will prepare will be based on whatever items are the best deals in the store. You are only shopping at your current store—you are not changing anything at this point; this is not a time to experiment. The learning curve you are on is pretty steep, so keep it as simple as you can. We will add more stores later, if you so desire.

Goal: Your main goal in the first three weeks is to come in as under-budget as possible, so that you will have extra cash to use for your stock-ahead items.

Example. If your budget is $200, you want to try to get all your needs in that week for no more than $175. This leaves you $25 to use for great deals for stocking ahead. The needs are the items you have to have: food for meals, produce, milk, and other things on your list you haven't stocked up on. Spend as little on these items as possible. Don't buy large and in bulk; buy small and spend less. You will stock up on these items later when they are a great deal. Just get enough to get you through until then.

Time. In the beginning, you will spend more time than you imagined organizing, planning, and clipping coupons. Don't be discouraged. Remember, you are on a gigantic learning curve. Be encouraged: you are doing the right thing. Stick with it; you will see results, and they are not far off.

WEEKS 5-8

$175 PER WEEK BUDGET

$150 TO MEET IMMEDIATE NEEDS	$25 TOWARD STOCK-UP ITEMS

Some of your weekly needs are being met from your previously purchased stock-up items.

Weeks 5-8: $175/week budget

After a month of having $25 a week to stock ahead with, you will begin to have some good staples on hand. This should allow you a little breathing room and more variety in your meal planning. In doing so, you will be able to spend less at the grocery on your "needs" items and allocate more of your budget to your "stock ahead" items. You can now reduce your weekly spending by $25, which will give you $125 or $150 to purchase "needs." This leaves you $25 to $50 for "stocking ahead" for each of the next four weeks.

Goal. Slightly reduce your total weekly spending as you are able. Every little bit helps, and seeing decreases in your weekly budget will encourage you to keep going toward even greater savings.

Example. Now your budget is at $175 a week, and you will be using your stockpile for the majority of your meal planning. The $150 will be to fill in the gaps and pick up the items you are running out of that you haven't been able to find on sale yet. How low you can get will determine just how much you will have to "stock ahead" with. The lower you can get your "needs," the more quickly you can reduce your overall budget and accumulate a nice stock of staples.

Time. Time involved and level of difficulty should both be decreasing now. You are getting more out of your planning time. Things are starting to click; you are getting it. Within just a few more weeks, you will have mastered the game of saving strategically.

WEEKS 9-12

$150 PER WEEK BUDGET

LESS AND LESS OF THE WEEKLY BUDGET TOWARD IMMEDIATE NEEDS	MORE AND MORE OF THE WEEKLY BUDGET TOWARD STOCK-UP ITEMS

More and more of your decreasing weekly budget is going toward finding great deals on stock-up items.

Weeks 9–12: $150/week budget

At this point you are really starting to rock and roll. You should be getting a better understanding of prices on the staples you purchase. The paradigm shift of "never paying full price" and stocking up on staples is becoming second nature to you. You're seeing the benefits of meal planning as you realize what being prepared can do. You might even be purchasing more weekly newspaper inserts to increase your savings. Also, you may be feeling comfortable enough to add another store or two to your weekly trips. Adding more stores will be a big advantage in getting the absolute best prices on your favorite items.

Goal. Your main goal at this stage is to take your knowledge and start being really strategic. Over the coming weeks, you will see a drastic reduction in your overall spending. What are you going to do with those extra savings? Use them to donate more items, add to your stockpile, or get a freezer for your garage.

Example. Now you are probably actually getting your needs in well under your weekly budget, and you have plenty of room in your budget to "stock ahead." Your grocery list is starting to look like the "Future" one we laid out earlier. Your needs are shrinking and the majority of the items on your list are just great deals you are finding to fill your pantry, refrigerator, and freezer.

Time. You are just about there on being more streamlined. At this point, you have figured out what does and doesn't work for you. You know what you should do to save time and money on each trip and in your weekly planning. Planning as you go is starting to make sense. You can see the light at the end of the tunnel. Hold on a little longer.

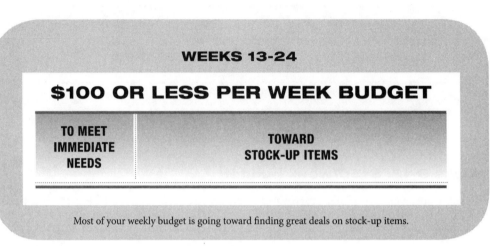

WEEKS 13-24

$100 OR LESS PER WEEK BUDGET

TO MEET IMMEDIATE NEEDS	TOWARD STOCK-UP ITEMS

Most of your weekly budget is going toward finding great deals on stock-up items.

Weeks 13–24: $100 or less per week budget

This has now become a new way of life for you—"Never pay full price" is your new mantra. The thought of paying full price for any item makes you cringe. Especially since you know that with just a little advance planning, you can probably find it on sale somewhere before you need it, or you can easily find a coupon. But at this point it isn't just about couponing at the grocery store; it is about implementing this lifestyle everywhere you shop.

Goal. A new way of life is your ultimate goal now. You are striving to implement this strategy of saving in every facet of what you do. It is becoming second nature for you to have restraint and self-control in your spending. It is not as much work at this point, and some days it is a game that you are playing against your checkbook!

LIVING *Generously* TIP

As you lower your monthly grocery budget with your new saving savvy lifestyle, look for opportunities to use that extra money to give to others.

Example. Now what does your life look like? At this point, your grocery budget should be close to reduced in half, and you have a lot less stress about your weekly grocery trips. You have a list in hand, grab what is on your list, snag a few clearance deals, and you are in and out of the store in close to thirty minutes for your week's shopping. Yes, you can really do that!

Time. Now that you are organized, know what you need, and know what is on sale, you can do all your planning in less than an hour total each week (this includes meal planning, the grocery list, coupons, and all). The trip itself is relatively short and now you feel comfortable snagging clearance deals; you know how to include them in your budget without going over. Improvising is not a big deal; you see the big picture. Take some items here, give some back there. It is all a balancing act with your budget.

Finally . . . Financial Freedom

Life is good. You are saving money. You are less stressed. You have more time for yourself. Your marriage is more stable because you aren't fighting about finances. I could keep going, but you need to find out for yourself what the joy of "never paying full price" again will do. It is the most freeing and satisfying thing in the entire world. Oh, and did I mention that you can give to others too?

. . . .

May [God] give you the desire of your heart
and make all your plans succeed.
PSALM 20:4

. . . .

For my husband and me, the most satisfying part of saving money has been being able to give to others. Now when I go to the grocery store, I am not only thinking about myself and my family, but I am also thinking about my community. A lifestyle of saving will inevitably lead to a lifestyle of giving when your heart is to bring glory to God.

I'll close with this blessing from the book of Ephesians:

> For this reason I kneel before the Father, from whom every family in heaven and on earth derives its name. I pray that out of his glorious riches he may strengthen you with power through his Spirit in your inner being, so that Christ may dwell in your hearts through faith. And I pray that you, being rooted and established in love, may have power, together with all the Lord's holy people, to grasp how wide and long and high and deep is the love of Christ, and to know this love that surpasses knowledge—that you may be filled to the measure of all the fullness of God.
>
> Now to him who is able to do immeasurably more than all we ask or imagine, according to his power that is at work within us, to him be glory in the church and in Christ Jesus throughout all generations, for ever and ever! Amen.
>
> Ephesians 3:14–21

FREQUENTLY ASKED QUESTIONS

Do you use coupons with non-sale items?

One of the first principles of using coupons strategically is to use them on sale items. The key to saving the maximum amount of money is to not be brand loyal and to purchase whatever product is on sale and that has a matching coupon. But as with anything, there are a few exceptions!

There are a few key items that I like and purchase whether on sale or not, and even if I don't have a coupon for them. There are two instances where I would use a coupon on a non-sale item:

1. *Item never goes on sale.* I will use a coupon on an item that I know never goes on sale. For instance, I have a favorite brand of salad dressing (a special flavor) and it never goes on sale. But I found a coupon for it. So the next time I went to the store I purchased it with the coupon, not on sale.

2. *Coupon is expiring.* If I have a high-value coupon for an item that my family prefers and the coupon is about to expire, I will go ahead and use it on a non-sale item. Sometimes the high-value coupons can create a "sale" type of price for the product.

Can you print coupons in black and white?

Yes! I never print my coupons in full color. As I described in chapter 5, here are a few of my favorite coupon printing tips.

- ◇ *Set printer default to black ink.* You need to set your printer's default to black ink only. You have to choose this as the computer default, because most computers print the coupons according to default settings, and you can't change the settings during printing.

◇ *Set print default to "fast or quick print."* There is no need to print coupons at a high-quality print setting; it is a waste of ink and money. Just make sure the setting is high enough that they will scan at checkout.

◇ *Print coupons on recycled paper.* I use the back of recycled paper to print my coupons. I have never had an issue at checkout with coupons having other text on the back side.

◇ *Recycle ink cartridges.* Pick your favorite office supply store and take in your empty ink cartridges to get "rewards" points to use in the store to purchase new ink packs.

I have my coupons grouped by expiration rather than category because I used to let them expire before using them. Is there a way to do it that's the best of both worlds?

As I describe in chapter 5, I personally feel like the most important element is having your coupons filed in such a way that you can easily find them for multiple purposes, not just expiring ones. It seems to me that to file by expiration date is only going to help you with the expiring coupons and it will probably frustrate you more to try to find the majority of your coupons on any given day.

Here is what I recommend:

◇ *Use a coupon database to find expired coupons.* If you want to make sure you are not missing out on the upcoming expiring coupons, you can use a coupon database to easily find them. All you do is go to FaithfulProvisions.com, search for Coupon Database under Coupons, and click on the "Expiration Date" tab until it gives you the most current date (see the arrow on the next page). Clicking here will list them all out by nearest expiration, and it will tell you where to find them too!

◇ *File favorite coupons up front.* Another method to use is to file all coupons by category and place your favorite coupons in the front pouch. Each time you do your grocery shopping you can flip through them to make sure you don't overlook them in the shuffle.

All in all, I feel like these are much better options than filing by expiration date, because you have more opportunity to use and easily find your coupons.

With Buy One Get One Free coupons, can you buy two products, use a BOGOF, and then another $1.00 off coupon? Also, if you have a Buy a Body Wash Get a Razor Free coupon, can you use that, plus a $1.00 off body wash, plus a $1.00 off a razor?

This can be tricky, but here is how it works:

Buy One Get One Free Coupons

When using a Buy One Get One Free (BOGOF) coupon, you can use one coupon for the item you are purchasing and then the BOGOF coupon for the free item, so you can use two coupons for the two items. Let me show you an example to help you visualize it.

> **Buy 2 Gillette Razors—on sale $1.99/ea**
> Use a BOGOF Gillette Razor coupon
> Use $1/1 Gillette Razor coupon
> **Final Price: $.99 for both razors**

You use the BOGOF coupon to get one free, so your total is at $1.99 for both razors. Then for the razor you paid for, you are using a $1/1 coupon, which brings your total down to 99 cents for both razors.

Buy One Item, Get a Different Item Free Coupons

On the second scenario you asked about, you can also only use two coupons. Here is how it would work:

> ### Buy Razor and Body Wash
> Use Buy Body Wash Get Razor Free coupon
> Use $1/1 Body Wash coupon
> ### Final Price: cost of body wash after $1 off

In this scenario, you again can only use one coupon on the free item, the one that got it free. So you can't use the coupon for the free razor and a $1/1 razor coupon too—use one or the other. Then you can use the $1/1 Body Wash coupon since the coupon was for the razor.

I hope that clears things up a bit! Just know that when using a BOGOF coupon, you can use another coupon on the item you paid full price for.

Now, after saying all that, you also need to know that this is also subject to the store manager's approval. If he says no, he is under no obligation to use them both.

I would love to know more about shopping for organic products. Are any of these items (for instance, natural sugars or whole wheat flours, organic produce, etc.) lower-priced at whole food stores rather than waiting for sales at regular grocery stores, which rarely have these items on sale?

I have to admit, this has been one of my greatest challenges. The main reason is because I have to make a shift in my budget total and in my mind-set when purchasing these types of items. While I can still find great deals on natural and organic products, they aren't as plentiful or frequent.

I have found the best way to save on organic and natural produce are the same concepts I use for conventional buys.

Stock ahead. I have to focus on stocking ahead on items we use a lot when they are on sale. For instance, when I see organic cereal on sale BOGOF (buy one get one free), I purchase enough to last me for up to six weeks if my budget will allow. If it is an expensive staple item, I focus on making those a majority of my budget that week. Check out chapter 2 for more stockpiling tips.

Flash-freeze fruits and veggies. One of my best tools to save big on organic produce and meats is my freezer. I flash-freeze lots of fruits and vegetables for things like blueberry-spinach smoothies and homemade soups. It is really easy to do. For more tips on flash-freezing, see chapter 3.

Use coupons. Nowadays, there are lots of organic and natural coupons. I have a full list of places you can print coupons on my "Organic and Natural Coupons" page on FaithfulProvisions.com. You can also search any product on my coupon database to find a specific coupon for a product you want to purchase. Each week I do coupon matchups with store sale items for stores like Whole Foods, Publix, and Kroger, who all carry their own lines of natural and organic products. Each frequently has store coupons and sales to match up with these products. For more information on using coupons, see chapter 5.

If a stockpile item is on sale for a great price and you have lots of coupons for that item, would you go over your grocery budget to stock up?

My first step would be to reevaluate what I already had on my list that I could eliminate to fit in the stockpiled item. For instance, if my budget is $100 per week, and aside from my "needs" most things on the list are stockpile items, I would prioritize my stockpile items to fit the most important (most expensive) items in first.

If most of the items on my list were needs and I had very little room for stock-up items, I would probably get rid of everything else on my list that was a stockpile item if this item was very important to me.

Here is how I prioritize:

- ◇ Is it a high-volume staple in our household?
- ◇ Is it an expensive staple?

- ◇ Are we completely out?

- ◇ Does it go on sale often?

- ◇ Are there coupons out for it frequently?

If it is not a high priority item according to the questions above, I try not to exceed my budget. The more you watch the sales cycles for the items you purchase, the more comfortable you will be letting a sale pass you by. Trust your planning and try not to make impulsive decisions that will exceed your budget.

I've recently noticed manufacturer coupons that say "Do Not Double." Does this mean that my store will not double them?

This question is a big topic of debate among my blog readers. The flat answer is that it depends on the store's policies. In my coupon usage, I have found that most stores double all coupons that fit their doubling criteria (e.g., 50 cents and under), even if the coupon says "Do Not Double" clearly on the top. In fact, I have even asked at my stores while at checkout and they say their store policy is to double that amount and that is what they will be doing!

The store is the one who actually covers the doubling cost and the reason the manufacturer usually puts that on the coupon is because they don't want to "devalue" their product with excessive discounting. The only store I have found not to double a "Do Not Double" coupon is Harris Teeter; all the other ones in my area double.

When you first began stockpiling, how much was your weekly grocery budget? How long did it take you to start seeing an opportunity to lower that?

- ◇ *Set a grocery budget.* First, you need to know what your grocery budget is going to be. Review your expenses versus your income to figure out at what amount you can afford to set your grocery budget. Once you have set your budget, you need to determine what goes on the list: your needs versus stock-ahead items.

- *List "needs" and "stock-up" items.* Each week when you do your grocery list, you will want to start with adding your "needs" to your list. Make out your meal plan according to what you already have on hand, and what is on sale in the store fliers that week. Your list should start with the staples you purchase each week, like milk, eggs, and produce, and then you add the items to round out your meal plan.

- *Use remaining budget for stocking up.* Add up all those things and see what your difference is: How much do you have left to work with? That would be your "stock-up" budget for that week. So, over the next few weeks what you will see is that the "need" items on the list will begin to shrink, which will allow you more of a budget to purchase your "stock-up" items.

- *Lower overall budget.* As you begin to create a stockpile, you can slowly start to decrease your budget a little every few weeks because you have most everything you need. Your "needs" on the list will begin to shrink and the majority of each week's budget will be spent on items that are a really good deal, at rock-bottom prices.

How long did it take you to get to $50 a week?

To get to your target grocery budget, whether it is $40 or $80, you must have your stockpile in place. For me it took a little time, around three to six months, but that is going to vary depending on your current financial situation. If you don't have a lot of extra money to work with, it will take you a little longer to stockpile, because you can't get as much of something when it is on sale.

Also, one thing to note: $50 a week won't work for everyone. If you have a large family, especially if they are big eaters, you will probably have to up your budget a little. Another thing that helps get you there is meal planning.

Now that you have a full pantry and freezer, how much do you pay for an item to stockpile (assuming you do not need it this week)? $2 or less? 60% off or less? What is a good guideline?

Since products vary in price and quality, I can't give you a specific dollar amount per item, but a percentage I shoot for is at least 50 percent. Now, there are some items we love that never go on sale. So, if I can get them for 30 percent off I am happy. The best way to know your prices is to keep a pricing sheet or notebook, and record where and what the best prices are that you find for particular items. In the beginning, I did a few shopping "field trips" to help me get an idea of standard pricing on our most purchased items.

If I wanted to, I could keep my weekly grocery budget at $100 a week. Between all the grocery stores and drugstores, I'm sure I could use all of this every week and not take the budget down. Any thoughts?

Do you *need* $100 of groceries each week? If the answer is yes, because you have a large family, special dietary needs, or you are using that budget to give and donate to a food pantry, then I say keep it there. I have found that my family of four can easily live on $50 a week if I am organized and disciplined. We will increase our budget or have a separate budget for baby items like formula and diapers, but for our main food staples, toiletries, and cleaning items, I can usually catch things on sale, on clearance, and with coupons to fit into our budget.

I'm trying to figure out how the couponing works when you're buying in bulk. Can I stack ten manufacturers' coupons (one per item) or is that too many? How do you know what the limit is?

You will have to call your specific store to see what their coupon policy is on maximum number of "like" coupons you can use per transaction. In my experience some stores have a limit of three.

A store told me for their buy one, get one free (BOGOF) offers, you can only use one manufacturer's coupon (MFC). It seems like other stores let you use two MFCs—one for each item. Does that sound right?

With BOGOF or Buy One Get One Free sales, if the store's policy is that you can buy one at 50 percent off, it makes perfect sense to use one coupon per item. However, in a store that has a policy where you must purchase both items to get the savings, it makes sense to only use one coupon. You need to check with your particular store to see their policies.

What if you see an item you want and you do not have the right hard copy issue of SS (Smart Source) or RP (RedPlum)? Can you get that coupon online somewhere? Also, are Internet coupons and hard copy coupons duplicates of each other (i.e., you either clip them or print them) or are they separate entities?

Typically when you find a coupon in your SS or RP (Smart Source or Red Plum) inserts, they are available somewhere on the Internet. But that doesn't guarantee that there is an IP (Internet printable) available. Just check out the Faithful Provisions coupon database to do a full search for online and in-print publications.

If you are using a competitor's store coupon, like a Food Lion coupon at Publix, can you use it for a store brand? (e.g., coupon for Food Lion brand diapers, can you use for Publix brand diapers)

Yes, actually you *should* use it for a store brand. Think of it this way, Publix takes Food Lion coupons because they would rather you buy their brand and stay at their store, than go to Food Lion to get one item cheaper. But as always, be sure to check with your store's customer service desk first.

Are there things you buy that tend to never have coupons?

Definitely, there are some items that never have coupons, but honestly I can't think of many! I have found all kinds of coupons, and lately I have found an abundance of organic coupons, which are a type of coupon many people search out. I have a page full of manufacturers that have organic coupons listed on FaithfulProvisions.com.

If FaithfulProvisions.com lists a coupon and where to find it, then you go to find it and the link doesn't work or the coupon isn't in the ad, is there a way to find the coupon they are referencing?

Coupons are regional, so sometimes coupons are listed in their regional list and then, for unknown reasons, the manufacturer decides to pull coupons from particular regions. I see that happen a lot. The only way to cross-reference is to try a coupon database.

MEAL-PLAN RECIPES

Easy Homemade Pizza Dough

    1 cup warm water (approximately 110° F)

    1 teaspoon sugar

    1 packet or 1 tablespoon active dry yeast

    2 tablespoons olive oil

    1 teaspoon salt

    1 cup whole wheat flour

    1½ cups + 2 tablespoons white flour

· · · · · · · · · ·

Easy Homemade
Pizza Dough

1. Preheat oven to 400° F.
2. Proof yeast (use water, sugar, and yeast) in a separate measuring cup.
3. Combine remaining ingredients, except flour, in large mixing bowl. Add yeast mixture.
4. Add flour and work in with a fork.
5. Once dough has formed into a pliable, non-sticky ball, remove it from bowl and place on floured surface. Knead and roll out with floured roller to fit onto pizza pan.
6. Bake for 15 minutes.

Bulk Pizza Dough
Recipe

Baked Ziti

    1 pound cooked, shaped pasta (ziti, bow-tie, penne, etc.)

    2 tablespoons fresh basil from garden (or 2 teaspoons dried basil)

    1 tablespoon garlic salt

    1 tub ricotta

1-2 (48-ounce) jars favorite spaghetti sauce

2 fresh roma tomatoes, diced

1 cup shredded mozzarella

Parmesan cheese

. . . .

1. Preheat oven to 350° F.

2. Cook pasta a few minutes less than the package directions call for, so it won't be mush after you cook it. Stir basil and garlic salt into ricotta and set aside.

3. Lightly layer the bottom of a casserole dish with sauce, then place approximately half of the pasta on top. Layer with all the ricotta mixture, Roma tomatoes, half of the sauce, more pasta and then the remaining sauce. Top with mozzarella.

4. Bake covered for 20 minutes, then uncovered for another 10 minutes. Serve with Parmesan cheese.

Chicken Pot Pie Soup

1 (10-count) package refrigerated biscuits or crescent rolls

Sweet paprika or chili powder (I prefer chili powder)

1½ pounds chicken breast pieces, diced

3 tablespoons butter

2 ribs celery and greens from the heart, chopped (I use the heart leaves too)

1 medium yellow onion, chopped

2 large carrots, peeled and diced

2 tablespoons Montreal Steak Seasoning

Salt and pepper

2 teaspoons poultry seasoning

3 tablespoons all-purpose flour

1 cup shredded potatoes (ready-to-cook-hash browns), available in sacks on dairy aisle

2 cups whole milk (or half & half or cream to make it thicker and creamier)

3 cups chicken stock

¼ teaspoon grated nutmeg (optional)

1 cup frozen green peas

. . . .

1. Preheat oven according to package directions and arrange biscuits on cookie sheet. (You might have biscuits left over. Save them for ham and cheese or egg and cheese breakfast sandwiches the next morning.) Sprinkle biscuits with a little paprika or chili powder and bake for 10 to 12 minutes.

2. Cut chicken into cubes.

3. In a medium pot over medium to medium-high heat, cook chicken in butter for 2 minutes, then add veggies, salt and pepper to taste, and poultry seasoning. (If you use the steak seasoning, do not add salt and pepper; it already has a lot!) Cook 5 minutes longer, add flour, cook another minute.

4. Add potatoes, then stir in whole milk, half and half, or cream, and chicken stock. Add nutmeg. Bring soup to a boil by raising heat, then turn heat back to simmer and cook soup another 10 minutes. Adjust seasonings. Stir in peas until heated through.
   TIP: If the soup is not thick enough for you, mix 1-2 tablespoons of flour with some of the warm liquid in a separate cup and mix until it has no lumps. (It will be a thick, gravy-like consistency.) Add to soup and stir. It will thicken within about 15 minutes.

Grilled Tilapia

1-2 pounds firm white fish (tilapia, grouper, cod)

2 tablespoons olive oil

1 tablespoon lemon pepper seasoning

. . . .

1. Place fish in a plastic bag and pour olive oil over the top, then sprinkle with lemon pepper seasoning.
2. Let marinate for 15 minutes.
3. Place fish in an aluminum pan and put on grill.
4. Cook about 3-4 minutes per side.

SERVING IDEAS:

Fish Sandwich

Fish Tacos

Main dish with rice and steamed broccoli

Fish Tacos

1-2 pounds white fish (cod, tilapia, grouper, mahi)

1 teaspoon lime juice

1 tablespoon olive oil

½ teaspoon each of cumin, coriander, and chili powder

Salt and pepper

Corn tortillas

Garnishes:

Cabbage or lettuce, thinly sliced

Green onions, chopped

Sour cream (add lime zest and lime juice to jazz it up!)

Fresh salsa

Lime juice

. . . .

1. Place fish in an aluminum pan and cover with: lime juice, olive oil, and spices. Grill in pan.
2. Heat corn tortillas in microwave for about 15 seconds.
3. Double them up and fill with fish, lettuce, sour cream, and salsa (we use the Aldi's Southwestern kind, yum!), and squirt lime juice over the contents.

Steak Marinade – All-Purpose Greek Marinade

⅓ cup olive oil

Juice of 2 lemons, or ⅓ cup lemon juice (I use the Minute-Maid Frozen Concentrate)

2 garlic cloves, minced (fresh is best!)

1 tablespoon oregano

1 tablespoon thyme

1 tablespoon basil

½ teaspoon kosher salt

½ teaspoon fresh ground pepper

. . . .

1. Mix all ingredients together in a jar and shake until well blended.
2. Pour over meat or vegetables.
3. For meat, marinate for 30 minutes to 1 hour. For vegetables, marinate 10-15 minutes.

Barbecue Chicken Pizza

Pizza dough (either refrigerated or homemade recipe from p. 197)

¼ cup barbecue sauce

1 cup cooked chicken

1 cup mozzarella or Monterey Jack shredded cheese

1 green or red pepper, sliced

¼ red or white onion, sliced

Cilantro

. . . .

1. Prepare pizza dough and prebake at 400° F for about 6 minutes.
2. Spread with barbecue sauce, and cover with toppings. Bake for another 10 minutes or until ready.
3. Garnish with cilantro.

Sirloin Pork Chops—Pork Chop Rub

2 tablespoons extra-virgin olive oil

2 tablespoons Worcestershire sauce

2 teaspoons cracked black pepper

2 teaspoons chili powder

2 teaspoons granulated garlic

2 teaspoons kosher salt

1 teaspoon cumin

½ teaspoon cinnamon

. . . .

1. Mix all ingredients together and rub on pork chops.
2. Let marinate for 1 hour or more.
3. Grill.

Chili Pot Roast

3-4 pounds of a favorite pot roast or flank steak

1 (12-ounce) jar chili sauce (I use Heinz)

1 large onion, sliced

. . . .

1. Combine ingredients in slow cooker.

2. Cook on low for 6-8 hours.

French Dip Sandwich

1 multigrain loaf of bread, sliced in half lengthwise

1 pound shredded beef (from pot roast)

2 tablespoons steak sauce

¼ cup shredded Monterey Jack or cheddar cheese

. . . .

1. Preheat oven to 350° F.

2. Lay sliced bread loaf on aluminum foil. Place beef inside, and top with sauce and cheese.

3. Wrap up and bake for 15-20 minutes or until warmed through.

Pizza Margherita

Pizza dough (either refrigerated or homemade recipe from p. 197)

Olive oil

Sliced garden or roma tomatoes

Shredded mozzarella

Fresh basil, chiffonade (To chiffonade, take all the leaves and stack them, then roll them up and slice them vertically to make thin strips)

Sea salt and cracked pepper

. . . .

1. Prebake dough according to directions, then remove from oven. Turn oven temperature up to 425° F.
2. Drizzle partially cooked dough with olive oil. Top with sliced tomatoes, shredded mozzarella, and basil.
3. Top with cracked pepper and sea salt to taste.
4. Bake at 425° F for 4-6 minutes.

Beef Empanadas

1 (8-ounce) package refrigerated pastry dough

2 cups chopped roast beef or leftover pot roast

1 (4-ounce) can diced green chiles

1 cup shredded cheese (I like Monterey Jack, but cheddar would be great)

. . . .

1. Let pastry dough come to room temperature for about 20 minutes before you try to roll it out.
2. Preheat oven to 425° F.
3. Lay out dough on a flat surface, one layer on top of another, and then use a pizza cutter to cut into quarters. You should have 8 pieces total.
4. Divide beef, chiles, and cheese evenly into quarters and place on 4 pastry pieces.

5. Top each with remaining pastry pieces and mash the edges with fingers, or press together with a fork.

6. Bake for 10-15 minutes or until golden brown.

** We eat two and freeze two (uncooked) for later. I layer them between sheets of wax paper to freeze and then place them in a freezer bag.

Pork Fried Rice

4 teaspoons canola or peanut oil, divided

2 eggs, beaten

2 garlic cloves, minced

2 carrots, diced or shredded

3 green onions, chopped

1 cup frozen peas

2 cups leftover rice (brown or white)

1 cup diced pork (precooked or leftover)

¼ cup hoisin or black bean sauce (or 4 tablespoons soy sauce)

. . . .

1. In a large skillet, heat 2 teaspoons of oil and scramble eggs. Remove from skillet and set aside.

2. Add remaining oil and sauté garlic and carrots for 2 minutes, then add onions, peas, rice, pork, and sauce. Stir. Add eggs back to mixture and stir well to break up eggs.

SERVING IDEAS:

Serve with fresh green salad or shredded carrot salad with ginger dressing.

PLANNING TEMPLATES

SAVINGS STRATEGIES TO-DO CHECKLIST

. . . .

IF YOU HAVE **MORE** TIME . . .

Chapter 2: Stocking Up

❏ **Make space and organize.** Clean out and organize your pantry.

❏ **Know your staple items.** Create a list of all your most frequently purchased items.

❏ **Buy seasonally.** Think ahead and plan to purchase seasonal items.

Chapter 3: Warming Up to the Freezer

❏ **Learn to flash-freeze foods.** This will help with ease of use and portion control.

❏ **Clean and organize your freezer.** You can maximize your savings if you have room to freeze and store all the great deals you will be getting.

❏ **Invest in a stand-alone freezer.** With a stand-alone freezer, you can really stock ahead with items you have saved a lot of money on.

Chapter 4: Planning Never Tasted So Good

❏ **Use ingredient-based recipes.** Plan your meals around the ingredients you have in your pantry and freezer.

❏ **Purchase kitchen appliances and tools.** Be sure to stock your kitchen with the proper items to help make your kitchen time more fruitful.

❏ **Manage meal planning.** Reference the sample weekly meal plans in this chapter, and use the template in the back of this book or at FaithfulProvisions.com to get you started.

Chapter 5: I've Got a Coupon for That

❏ **Clip and file coupons.** Having more time will allow you to save more by clipping all coupons and filing them so you can take them to the store to grab missed sale and clearance items.

- ❑ **Stack manufacturer and store coupons.** When an item is on sale, stack a manufacturer coupon with a store coupon to save the most.
- ❑ **Host a coupon swap.** A great way to get extra coupons for free and donate your unused ones is to either attend or host a coupon swap in your area.
- ❑ **Use a coupon clipping service.** If you are out of time, or want to stock up on a particular item, use a coupon clipping service to get more coupons for the items you want.
- ❑ **Read blog comments.** When you are on a blog that does coupon matchups or deals, be sure to read through the readers' comments. There are usually lots of gems found in there!

Chapter 7: The Grocery Trip

- ❑ **Shop multiple stores.** If you are able, shopping the sales at multiple stores will save you more money.
- ❑ **Fill a shopping tote.** Get a shopping tote and fill it with all the things you will need for each shopping trip.
- ❑ **Know your store.** Before you shop, call your store and look online for their policies and loyalty programs.
- ❑ **Use a shopping list template.** Create your own template or use the downloadable Grocery Shopping List template on FaithfulProvisions.com before you hit the store.

IF YOU HAVE *LESS* TIME . . .

Chapter 2: Stocking Up

- ❑ **Use a price list.** Print out or download the Provisions Price List from FaithfulProvisions.com to reference when you are shopping.
- ❑ **Start stocking up.** When your favorite items go on sale, buy extras so you never pay full price.

Chapter 3: Warming Up to the Freezer

- ❑ **Use proper storage techniques.** Use the right containers to store your food in the freezer.
- ❑ **Purge your freezer.** Discard what you don't need and make room for the great deals you will find.
- ❑ **Create a Freezer Inventory List.** Download the Freezer Inventory List from FaithfulProvisions.com, photocopy it from the back of this book, or create your own to keep track of what's in your freezer.

Chapter 4: Planning Never Tasted So Good

- ❏ **Plan around your calendar.** Be sure to meal plan around your schedule. Many times you don't need a meal every night.
- ❏ **Use a meal-planning service.** Use a service like E-Mealz.com to make your meal planning easy!
- ❏ **Know your "go-to" meals.** Create a list of your family's favorite meals and keep supplies on hand for those meals.
- ❏ **Use the slow cooker.** If you don't have a slow cooker, it's worth the investment. The easiest meal planning tool is putting things in the cooker and letting it cook all day, so dinner is ready when you come home.
- ❏ **Be creative with leftovers.** Use what is in your fridge to save money and time.

Chapter 5: I've Got a Coupon for That

- ❏ **Buy store brands.** If you can't find a coupon to go with a sale item, sometimes you are better off just purchasing the store brand.
- ❏ **Use coupons for sale items.** The best way to use coupons is in conjunction with a sale item.
- ❏ **Use a coupon database.** Use a coupon database to easily and quickly find the coupons you are looking for either online, in Sunday coupon inserts, or in coupon booklets.
- ❏ **File coupons by insert.** If you are looking to save time, file your Sunday coupon inserts and booklets by date or topic. Then use the coupon database to easily find them.
- ❏ **Know store policies.** Before heading to your store, make sure you know their policies on things like BOGOF items and doubling coupons. This prevents a lot of stress at the checkout lane.
- ❏ **Learn coupon lingo.** One of the most important things to know are the abbreviations you will see on blogs and coupon matchup sites. Print the list off and keep it handy, no memorizing needed!

Chapter 7: The Grocery Trip

- ❏ **Set a shopping day.** Establish a shopping day as part of your routine.
- ❏ **Shop one store.** If you are low on time, you can save greatly by just sticking with one store. It takes a little longer, but can easily be done.
- ❏ **Read store ads.** While you are shopping, make sure you have a store ad in hand at all times to verify product, sizes, varieties, and price.
- ❏ **Use rain checks.** If your store is out of an item, grab a rain check so you can get it next time.
- ❏ **Check your receipt.** Before you walk out of the store, check your receipt to make sure the total is correct. If not, you can fix it at customer service, preventing extra trips.

faithful provisions

Meal Plan Calendar

Week Of

month | day

Dinner			
Sunday ☐ DINE IN ☐ DINE OUT ☐ TAKEOUT	**Breakfast**
Monday ☐ DINE IN ☐ DINE OUT ☐ TAKEOUT	
Tuesday ☐ DINE IN ☐ DINE OUT ☐ TAKEOUT	**Lunches**
Wednesday ☐ DINE IN ☐ DINE OUT ☐ TAKEOUT	
Thursday ☐ DINE IN ☐ DINE OUT ☐ TAKEOUT	**Snacks**
Friday ☐ DINE IN ☐ DINE OUT ☐ TAKEOUT	
Saturday ☐ DINE IN ☐ DINE OUT ☐ TAKEOUT	

save money. live generously.

faithful provisions

Freezer Inventory

Item	Qty	Location	Item	Qty	Location
Meats:			Fruits & Veggies:		
Prepared Meals:					
			Desserts:		
			Misc:		
Breads:					

save money. live generously.

faithful provisions

Weekly Grocery Budget List

Store: ....
Total $ ....

Quantity	Item (Coupons)	Total Cost

save money. live generously.

faithful provisions

Grocery List

Fruits & Veggies
- ☐ Apples
- ☐ Avocado
- ☐ Blueberries
- ☐ Broccoli
- ☐ Carrots
- ☐ Celery
- ☐ Cucumber
- ☐ Grapes
- ☐ Lemons/Limes
- ☐ Lettuce
- ☐ Melon
- ☐ Onions
- ☐ Oranges
- ☐ Peppers
- ☐ Potatoes
- ☐ Spinach
- ☐ Tomatoes
- ☐ Salad Mix
- ☐ Strawberries
- ☐ ....
- ☐ ....

Deli
- ☐ Lunch Meat
- ☐ Cheese
- ☐ Breads
- ☐ Salads
- ☐ ....
- ☐ ....

Meats
- ☐ Chicken
- ☐ Turkey
- ☐ Hamburger
- ☐ Pork Chops
- ☐ Pork Roast
- ☐ Pork Tenderloins
- ☐ Beef Roast
- ☐ Steak
- ☐ Fish
- ☐ Bacon
- ☐ Sausage
- ☐ ....
- ☐ ....

Breakfast
- ☐ Cereal
- ☐ Oatmeal
- ☐ ....

Canned/Boxed Goods
- ☐ Applesauce
- ☐ Broth
- ☐ Corn
- ☐ Fruit Cocktail
- ☐ Green Beans
- ☐ Mushrooms
- ☐ Jello
- ☐ Peas
- ☐ Peaches
- ☐ Pineapple
- ☐ Pizza Sauce
- ☐ Pudding
- ☐ Raisins
- ☐ Soup
- ☐ Spaghetti Sauce
- ☐ Tomato Sauce/Paste
- ☐ Tomatoes
- ☐ Tuna
- ☐ ....
- ☐ ....

Pasta
- ☐ Spaghetti
- ☐ Lasagna
- ☐ Rice
- ☐ ....
- ☐ ....

Frozen
- ☐ Waffles
- ☐ Pizza
- ☐ Chicken Nuggets
- ☐ Vegetables
- ☐ Potatoes
- ☐ Dinner Bread
- ☐ ....
- ☐ ....

Bread
- ☐ Bread Loaf
- ☐ English muffins
- ☐ Bagels
- ☐ Buns
- ☐ ....
- ☐ ....

Snack Foods
- ☐ Chips
- ☐ Cookies
- ☐ Popcorn
- ☐ Crackers
- ☐ Granola Bars
- ☐ ....
- ☐ ....

Condiments
- ☐ Ketchup
- ☐ Mustard
- ☐ Mayonnaise
- ☐ Pickles
- ☐ Salad Dressing
- ☐ Peanut Butter
- ☐ Jelly
- ☐ Pancake Syrup
- ☐ ....
- ☐ ....

Ethnic Foods
- ☐ Soy Sauce
- ☐ Teriyaki Sauce
- ☐ Taco Seasoning
- ☐ Tortillas
- ☐ Tacos
- ☐ Wontons
- ☐ ....
- ☐ ....

Baby Items
- ☐ Formula
- ☐ Baby Food
- ☐ Diapers
- ☐ Wipes

Baking Goods
- ☐ Flour
- ☐ Sugar
- ☐ Salt
- ☐ Pepper
- ☐ Pancake Mix
- ☐ Cake Mix
- ☐ Brownies
- ☐ Chocolate Chips
- ☐ ....
- ☐ ....

Beverages
- ☐ Juice
- ☐ Bottled Water
- ☐ Soft Drinks
- ☐ Lemonade
- ☐ Coffee
- ☐ Tea
- ☐ ....
- ☐ ....

Dairy
- ☐ Milk
- ☐ Eggs
- ☐ Cheese
- ☐ Yogurt
- ☐ Butter
- ☐ Cream Cheese
- ☐ Sour Cream
- ☐ Cottage Cheese
- ☐ Coffee Creamer

Paper Products
- ☐ Napkins
- ☐ Paper Towels
- ☐ Tissues
- ☐ Toilet Paper
- ☐ Garbage Bags
- ☐ Aluminum Foil
- ☐ Wax Paper
- ☐ Plastic Wrap

Cleaning Products
- ☐ Dish Soap
- ☐ Hand Soap
- ☐ Dishwashing Detergent
- ☐ Laundry Detergent
- ☐ Fabric Softener
- ☐ Window Claner
- ☐ Sponges Brushes
- ☐ Wipes

Other
- ☐ ....
- ☐ ....
- ☐ ....
- ☐ ....

save money. live generously.

faithful provisions Food Substitution List

If you don't have:	Substitute:
Bacon, 1 slice	1 Tbs. cooked bacon pieces
Baking Powder, 1 tsp.	1/2 tsp. cream of tartar + 1/4 tsp. baking soda
Baking Soda	There is no substitute for baking soda.
Balsamic Vinegar, 1 Tbs.	1 Tbs. cider vinegar or red wine vinegar + 1/2 tsp. sugar
Bread crumbs, fine dry, 1/4 cup	3/4 cup soft bread crumbs, or 1/4 cup cracker crumbs, or 1/4 cup cornflake crumbs
Brown Sugar, 1 cup	1 cup white sugar + 4 Tbs. molasses
Broth, beef or chicken, 1 cup	1 tsp. or 1 cube instant beef or chicken bouillon + 1 cup hot water
Butter, 1 cup	1 Tbs. shortening + 1/4 tsp. salt, if desired
Buttermilk, 1 cup	1 tbs. Lemon juice or vinegar + enough milk to make 1 cup (let stand 5 minutes before using)
Chocolate, semisweet, 1 ounce	3 Tbs. semisweet chocolate pieces, or 1 Tbs. unsweetened cocoa powder +2 tsp. sugar and 2 tsp. shortening
Chocolate, sweet baking, 4 ounces	1/4 cup unsweetened cocoa powder + 1/3 cup granulated sugar and 3 Tbs. shortening
Chocolate, unsweetened, 1 ounce	3 Tbs. unsweetened cocoa powder + 1 Tbs. cooking oil, or shortening melted
Cornstarch, 1 Tbs. (for thickening)	2 Tbs. all-purpose flour
Corn syrup (light), 1 cup	1 cup granulated sugar + 1/4 cup water
Cream (whipping), 1 cup unwhipped	2 cups prepared whipping cream (1 cup unwhipped = 2 cups whipped)
Garlic, 1 clove	1/2 tsp. bottles minced garlic or 1/8 tsp. garlic powder
Ginger, grated fresh, 1 tsp.	1/4 tsp. ground ginger
Half-and-Half or light cream, 1 cup	1 Tbs. Melted butter + enough whole milk to make 1 cup
Fresh Herbs, 1 Tbs.	1 tsp. dried leaf herbs or 1/2 tsp ground dried
Flour (All-Purpose White)	1/2 cup whole wheat flour plus 1/2 cup all-purpose flour (no more than 1/2 and 1/2 when you use whole wheat)
Flour (self-Rising)	1 cup minus 2 tsp all-purpose flour + 1 1/2 tsp baking powder and 1/2 tsp salt
Mayonnaise, 1 cup	1 cup sour cream, 1 cup yogurt, 1 cup cottage cheese (in blender or processor) OR use any for part of the mayonnaise
Molasses, 1 cup	1 cup honey
Mustard, dry, 1 tsp.	1 Tbs. prepared mustard
Onion, chopped, 1/2 cup	2 Tbs. dried minced onion or 1/2 tsp. onion powder
Rum, 1/4 cup	1 Tbs. rum extract plus 3 Tbs. water
Sour cream, dairy, 1 cup	1 cup plain yogurt
Sugar, granulated, 1 cup	1 cup packed brown sugar or 2 cups sifted powdered sugar, or 7/8 cup honey
Sugar, powdered, 1 cup	1 cup granulated sugar + 1 Tbs. cornstarch; process in a food processor using the metal blade attachment until it's well blended and powdery.
Tomato Juice, 1 cup	1/2 cup tomato sauce + 1/2 cup water
Tomato sauce, 2 cups	3/4 cup tomato paste + 1 cup water
Wine, red, 1 cup	1 cup beef or chicken broth in savory recipes; cranberry juice in desserts
Wine, white, 1 cup	1 cup chicken broth in savory recipes; apple juice or white grape juice in desserts
Yeast, active dry, 1 package	About 2 1/4 tsp. active dry yeast

 save money. live generously.

faithful provisions

Seasonal Fruit & Veggies

Winter	Spring	Summer	Fall
December, January, February	March, April, May	June, July, August	September, October, November
Avocados	Asparagus	Apricots	Apples
Broccoli	Avocados	Basil	Broccoli
Brussels Sprouts	Basil	Beans	Brussel Sprouts
Cabbage	Beans	Beets	Cabbage
Chinese Cabbage	Beets	Berries	Chinese Cabbage
Cauliflower	Berries	Cherries	Cauliflower
Celery Root	Broccoli	Corn	Celery Root
Chicory	Cabbage	Cucumbers	Chicory
Fennel	Chinese Cabbage	Dates	Cranberries
Grapefruit	Cucumbers	Figs	Cucumbers
Greens	Radish	Grapes	Dates
Wild Mushrooms	Head or Iceberg Lettuce	Mangoes	Fennel
Mandarin Oranges	Mangoes	Melons	Grapes
Sweet Oranges	Okra	Okra	Greens
Pears	Sweet Oranges	Peaches	Head or Iceberg Lettuce
Spinach	Papayas	Chile Peppers	Leaf Lettuce
Sweet Potatoes	Peas	Sweet Peppers	Mushrooms
	Chile Peppers	Plums	Nuts
	Sweet Peppers	Summer Squash	Okra
	Rhubarb	Tomatoes	Mandarin Oranges
	Shallots	Watermelon	Pears
	Spinach		Chile Peppers
	Summer Squash		Sweet Peppers
	Turnips		Persimmons
			Pomegranates
			Quince
			Shallots
			Spinach
			Winter Squash
			Star Fruit
			Sweet Potatoes

save money. live generously.

faithful provisions

Prep Day Planner

Recipe Ideas

Prep List

Shopping List

Notes:

save money. live generously.
www.faithfulprovisions.com

Notes

Chapter 1: Save Money, Live Generously

1. Dennis Jacobe, "U.S. Underemployment Steady at 18.4% in July," Gallup.com, August 5, 2010, http://www.gallup.com/poll/141770/underemployment-steady-july.aspx.

2. James Rankin and Kyle Brown, "Personal Income and Outlays, January 2011," US Department of Commerce, Bureau of Economic Analysis, February 28, 2011, http://www.bea.gov/newsreleases/national/pi/pinewsrelease.htm.

3. Teresa Mears, "Expect Higher Food Prices This Year," MSN.com, January 26, 2011, http://money.msn.com/saving-money-tips/post.aspx?post=9c4bb9c1-06d4-4c9d-83f9-1b5e29186485.

4. Nathan A. Martin, "Total U.S. Savings Rate Lowest in Recorded History," Wall Street Pit, January 6, 2010, http://wallstreetpit.com/13428-total-us-savings-rate-lowest-in-recorded-history

5. Associated Press, "1.6 million more Americans volunteered in 2009," *USA Today*, June 15, 2010, http://www.usatoday.com/news/nation/2010-06-15-more-americans-volunteered_N.htm

6. Ben Woolsey and Matt Schulz, "Credit card statistics, industry facts, debt statistics," CreditCards.com, http://www.creditcards.com/credit-card-news/credit-card-industry-facts-personal-debt-statistics-1276.php.

7. Laura McGann, "Coupons Make a Comeback: Redemption Up 27%," Neiman Journalism Lab, February 10, 2010, http://www.niemanlab.org/2010/02/coupons-make-a-comeback-redemption-up-27/.

8. Dictionary.com, s.v. "savvy," http://dictionary.reference.com/browse/savvy. Copyright © 2011 Dictionary.com, LLC. All rights reserved.

Chapter 2: Preparing Your Pantry

1. Karen Ehman, *The Complete Guide to Getting and Staying Organized* (Eugene, OR: Harvest House, 2008), 148.

Chapter 4: Planning Never Tasted So Good

1. Better Homes and Gardens, *Better Homes and Gardens New Cookbook*, 15th edition (Hoboken, NJ: Wiley Books, 2010).

2. Ree Drummond, *The Pioneer Woman Cooks: Recipes from an Accidental Country Girl* (New York: William Morrow, 2009).

3. Giada de Laurentiis, *Giada's Family Dinners* (New York: Clarkson Potter, 2006). This is just one of her many good cookbooks—I like them all!

4. Stephanie O'Dea, *Make It Fast, Cook It Slow: The Big Book of Everyday Slow Cooking* (New York: Hyperion, 2009).

5. Lisa Lillien, *Hungry Girl 1-2-3: The Easiest, Most Delicious, Guilt-Free Recipes on the Planet* (New York: St. Martin's Griffin, 2010). Lisa (aka "Hungry Girl") has several great cookbooks to choose from.

6. Ina Garten, *Barefoot Contessa How Easy Is That?: Fabulous Recipes and Easy Tips* (New York: Clarkson Potter, 2010). Cookbooks by Ina (aka "the Barefoot Contessa") are a staple in many kitchens, providing simple, delicious meals that almost anyone can prepare.

Chapter 5: I've Got a Coupon for That!

1. Denise Topolnicki, *How to Raise a Family on Less than Two Incomes* (New York: Broadway, 2001), 184.

2. "How Do Store Coupons Work?" *How Stuff Works*, http://money.howstuffworks.com/personal-finance/budgeting/question426.htm

3. John C. Maxwell, *There's No Such Thing as "Business" Ethics* (Nashville, TN: Center Street, 2003), 13

4. http://www.hotcouponworld.com/forums/its-got-real/.

WORTHY

PUBLISHING

IF YOU LIKED THIS BOOK . . .

- Tell your friends by going to: http://saving-savvy.com/ and clicking "LIKE"

- Share the video book trailer by posting it on your Facebook page

- Head over to our Facebook page, click "LIKE" and post a comment regarding what you enjoyed about the book

- Tweet "I recommend reading #SavingSavvy @SavingSavvyBook"

- Hashtag: #SavingSavvy

- Subscribe to our newsletter by going to http://worthypublishing.com/about/subscribe.php

- Connect with Kelly by following her on twitter @faithfulprov or @SavingSavvyBook and on Facebook at www.facebook.com/faithfulprovisions or www.facebook.com/savingsavvybook

Worthy Publishing
Facebook Page

Worthy Publishing
Website

Kelly Hancock left a successful career in the corporate world to stay at home and raise a family. In the process of adjusting to a radical drop in household income, she discovered a treasure trove of secrets and strategies for saving money, buying smart and experiencing the joy of giving. She began a blog—FaithfulProvisions.com—that became wildly popular, receiving thousands of visitors each week. Kelly is now a frequent guest on radio and television programs. She and her husband, Bradford, have two children and live in Nashville, Tennessee.